Transparently, cautiously,
for God's presence, mining the Bible as well as
tors for help along the way. To anyone who experiences pain, depression, confusion, or simply a nagging sense of life's unfairness, I recommend Michele Cushatt as a trustworthy guide.

—Philip Yancey, bestselling author

In *Relentless,* you'll be reminded of the only one who never falls short but meets you in your darkness and gives you hope. Through Michele's remarkable story of survival, you'll encounter the real Jesus, who is near to the brokenhearted and is faithful and true in our weakness and need.

—Kelly M. Rosati, CEO, KMR Consulting; child advocate

Michele explores God's utter faithfulness amid unrelenting pain and inexplicable circumstances. Pretty much everyone I know is walking through a storm or loves someone who is. Which means everyone needs this book. Read it slowly. Take it in. Your soul will be richer for it.

—Susie Larson, talk show host; speaker; author, *Fully Alive*

I wept as I read this book. I thought I'd skim it, but it wouldn't let me go. It is brutally honest and achingly human. If you have ever struggled to find God in your pain, Michele has given us a roadmap. *Relentless* will shake your faith to the core, and what you will be left with will be real and pure and hope and Jesus.

—Sheila Walsh, author, *Praying Women*

Michele Cushatt is a rare gem, courageously honest about the raw anguish of her reality while declaring the steadfast beauty of her savior. Michele's vulnerability strips away every Christian cliche and dives into the gut-wrenching search for a God who never leaves us. This book will challenge you and change you!

—Dr. Juli Slattery, psychologist; author, *Rethinking Sexuality*

Cushatt takes our hand and walks with us through the big question many of us don't dare ask while suffering, but think all the same: "Why have You forsaken me?" Along the way, she deftly interweaves her testimony with an examination of Scripture, guiding us to recognize, remember, and rest in God's relentless presence.

—Alia Joy, author, *Glorious Weakness*

In *Relentless*, Michele Cushatt invites us to lay bare our fears and disappointments, our emotional heartaches and physical struggles, so the sweet balm of truth can do its healing work. No pat answers or easy solutions here. Only hard-earned wisdom from a woman who longs for us to experience the presence of a God who never lets go.

—Liz Curtis Higgs, author, *Bad Girls of the Bible*

With a deep understanding of the questions that arise in the mind and heart of the person who wants to believe God but is struggling to do so, Michele provides a firm path of faith, plowed by her own wrestling and smoothed by the answers she fought to find. If the pain you've experienced has caused you to question God's power or His love, Michele knows. And she's written this book for you.

—Chrystal Evans Hurst, author and speaker

RELENTLESS

OTHER BOOKS BY MICHELE CUSHATT

I Am: A Sixty-Day Journey to Knowing Who You Are because of Who He Is

Undone: A Story of Making Peace with an Unexpected Life

RELENTLESS

THE UNSHAKEABLE PRESENCE OF A GOD WHO NEVER LEAVES

MICHELE CUSHATT

ZONDERVAN

Relentless

Requests for information should be addressed to:
Zondervan, *3900 Sparks Dr. SE, Grand Rapids, Michigan 49546*

Zondervan titles may be purchased in bulk for educational, business, fundraising, or promotional use. For information, please email SpecialMarkets@Zondervan.com.

ISBN 978-0-310-35299-0 (softcover)

ISBN 978-0-310-35820-6 (audio)

ISBN 978-0-310-35302-7 (ebook)

Published in association with the literary agency of Wolgemuth & Associates, Inc.

Cover design: James W. Hall IV
Cover photos: Tara Romasanta Photography / Kelly Knox / Stocksy
Interior design: Denise Froehlich

Printed in the United States of America

19 20 21 22 23 LSC 10 9 8 7 6 5 4 3 2 1

I will not leave you as orphans; I will come to you.

—JOHN 14:18

Contents

INTRODUCTION

The Twelve Stones

This is a dark world. There are many ways we keep that darkness at bay, but we cannot do it forever. Eventually the lights of our lives—love, health, home, work—will begin to go out. And when that happens, we will need something more than what our own understanding, competence, and power can give us.

—TIMOTHY KELLER, *WALKING WITH GOD THROUGH PAIN AND SUFFERING*

APRIL 2015

DENVER, COLORADO

The last of the light glinted off the glass.

Maker's Mark Kentucky Straight Bourbon Whisky. Handmade.

A gift to my husband months before. From whom? That guy from work, maybe. Didn't matter.

My hand—bone thin, old—reached for the glass neck, considering.

The other hand held another bottle. Smaller. Plastic. With a pharmacist's white and yellow label. No light danced like diamonds on its shell.

I held it tightly. Although I hated it, I needed it. Liquid morphine doled out in the smallest of portions every three to four hours when the burns and cancer pain grew Goliathlike and untamable by the various other potions poisoning my body.

I looked at both bottles, shameful thoughts swirling in my head. Unspeakable thoughts.

I should be upstairs, I remember thinking. My hands shook.

I flipped off the lights, uncomfortable in their glare. Even in the dark, I knew my reality was not normal. A forty-three-year-old mama is supposed to spend her days driving kids to baseball practice and gymnastics lessons. Walking them to the bus stop and helping them with their homework. Making heaping platters of spaghetti and fresh batches of chocolate chip cookies. Loving her husband and sharing secrets with him under the stars.

I could do none of those things. Instead, I spent my days stumbling from the couch to the toilet and back. Crying out for my husband to help, to keep me from choking on my vomit or to help me clean up my mess. A walk to the bus stop was out of the question.

I curled up in the dark of our basement, far from the life I once lived upstairs.

God, oh God, where are You?

Like a girl looking at the sun but unable to feel its warmth, I could no longer watch the beauty of life when I could experience none of it for myself. So I buried myself in the basement, my grave. The pain was too great. I was buried alive, trapped in a body that no longer worked.

Looking for God but unable to find Him.

Death beat at my door. So be it. Hadn't I endured enough? This was no way to live.

I looked again at the two bottles. Footsteps danced across the floor above me, so many of them. My husband, our children. The family I'd always wanted and prayed for. The family now compromised by cancer and a swallowing despair.

They already felt out of reach for me.

But relief sat within the grasp of my two hands. No more suffering. No more darkness. No more writhing in agony wishing for Death to set me free.

Fifteen minutes? Maybe less. Then it would all be over.

The last of the light glinted off the glass.

I've spent the better part of three years trying to decide whether I should tell you that story. I'm still not convinced of my decision. That night, I'd reached the end of myself. Three bouts of head and neck cancer—on top of too many other losses in the years before—had delivered overwhelming pain and defeat, obliterating my bulldog determination.

It wasn't that I wanted to die. I simply couldn't bear the thought of living.

In the process of saving my life from cancer, surgeons removed two-thirds of my tongue, multiple lymph nodes, and my submandibular gland. Then to rebuild the mouth and neck they had destroyed, the same surgeons removed tissue and blood vessels from my neck and left arm—wrist to elbow—and skin from my left thigh. All of these pieces and parts were used to put this Humpty Dumpty back together again. Only, in the end, I had burns from nose to chest, scars on much of my body, a feeding tube for five months, a tracheostomy for two months, ongoing chronic pain, and a body that would never look or function the same again.

Mine was, initially, a physical pain, the kind of suffering that required months of twenty-four-hour-a-day fentanyl—an opioid narcotic up to fifty times more potent than heroin—along with its less potent sidekick, liquid morphine, to take the edge off. Not to mention megadoses of steroids and antiemetics to stem the constant nausea and vomiting.[1]

None delivered relief.

What complicated my physical suffering were the emotional wounds and the unanswered questions. Where was God? I'd followed Him my whole life, loved Him with every breath. And yet the unyielding nature of my suffering, in spite of the prayers of thousands for relief, baffled me.

God, why won't You do something? Did I do something wrong? Are You mad at me?

He didn't answer. And His silence devastated me.

I feared I'd been abandoned by the God I'd always loved. Or worse, that the God I'd always believed in wasn't real after all. The years of fighting for life sapped my strength and my faith, and I felt myself giving up.

That wasn't the last time despair almost got the best of me. I could use up all of my fingers and toes counting the number of days in the last three years when the thought of ending my life seemed like an option. The reasons for this are many, not the least of which are the physical dues I pay each day for having almost died and yet lived: muscle tightness, atrophy, and diminished mobility in my neck from radiation and multiple surgical scars, inside and out. Compromised saliva production and the resulting dry mouth and difficulty eating. Near constant mouth, throat, and neck pain. Radiation burns and scarring inside my mouth and down through my throat, making it difficult to eat and swallow. Daily choking. A thyroid gland so burned by radiation that it no longer works and a metabolic system that struggles to regulate with medication replacement. And the chronic fatigue of a body taxed by the daily struggle to function in a compromised capacity.

And I haven't yet tallied the emotional toll.

I consistently fight a diminished will to live. Like King Solomon, I've often cried, "Utterly meaningless! Everything is meaningless" (Eccl. 1:2).

It sobers me, now, to think how close I crawled to the edge. To survive cancer and yet almost succumb to the cure of it. We pay such a steep price to preserve life.

Even so, I look at the woman buried in her despair with compassion. Her suffering was more than any human should bear. And her faith questions came from a valid place.

Perhaps you don't understand how a professing Christian could despair of life and wrestle with her faith. You may have climbed already to higher ground, a perch from which you shake your head at my weak spirituality.

I get it. I once thought the same.

If that's your position, this book is not for you. Not yet. My words are for those who find their faith flagging, their fear fanning. It's for the men and women who feel beat up by a faith that has failed them and a God who has disappointed them. It's for those who doubt but desperately want to believe.

Sometimes you can't bootstrap yourself to health. Sometimes, broken is all you have to offer.

As Ann Voskamp penned in her book *The Way of Abundance*, "Sometimes you can't help where you're broken, you can't help how the story turned out, you can't help how things fell apart and you got banged and busted up. And shame about the things you can't help—helps you the least . . . Maybe on the days we want out of our lives, it isn't so much that we want to die from shame as hide from shame."[2]

Author Brennan Manning said he was often asked how it was possible that he became an alcoholic after he was saved. His answer? "It is possible because I got battered and bruised by loneliness and failure; because I got discouraged, uncertain, guilt-ridden, and took my eyes off Jesus."[3]

Yes. That.

What proved the most dangerous to my faith in these years of despair wasn't cancer or crisis. It was the theological inaccuracies that had infiltrated my faith in childhood, perpetuated by other flawed, faith-hungry humans like me.

A single degree of error goes unnoticed in the first miles of a journey, but the longer you travel, the more off course you end up. The first signs showed up in my twenties and thirties when I faced an unexpected divorce and single motherhood. By the time the first cancer diagnosis hit in my late thirties and forties, my faith was so far off course that I was lost.

This is why I dare to tell this story. I recognize the risk of disclosing my ugly truth. Some might struggle to understand how I ended up here; others might judge, criticize, and reject. I have enough pride to reconsider. Even so, something far more important than my reputation compels me.

You.

The one who, moments ago, read of my despair and discovered, to your deep relief, you're not the only one who feels swallowed up by the dark.

You, the one drowning in impossible questions that threaten to take down your faith.

You, the truth seeker who simply wants to know whether the God she's heard about isn't an illusion or the product of wishful thinking.

You, the faithful follower who fears that your pain and losses are proof that God is disappointed in you, angry with you, and has left you.

And, yes, for you, the untried Jesus follower who hasn't yet faced the worst and doesn't realize she may be walking around theologically off course even now.

This is the necessary and perhaps ambitious quest of this book. To descend into the basement of my faith journey and, hopefully, discover evidence of God's presence. To scour the sixty-six books of the Bible for glimmers of God's never-ending desire to be with us. To learn, once and for all, that God doesn't condemn our questions, doubts, and despair but actually pushes further in, drawing closer still. And to discover, to our deep relief and lasting delight, that

God's greatest desire isn't to browbeat us into obedience but to woo us with His relentless nearness.

THE PROBLEM

I've come to recognize the near universality of the "Where is God?" question. It is a question asked in the day and in the night by skeptics and believers alike. Behind the question sits a fear more crushing than any other pain.

The fear of being alone.

Although both physical and relational pain can alter a life, the latter is more devastating. The first threatens the body; the second threatens the soul.

Humans can have great courage when buoyed by relationship. A woman can bear the agony of unmedicated childbirth multiple times with her husband holding her hand. A frightened ten-year-old will leap into a pool of frigid water from a twenty-foot cliff—a distance multiple times his height—as long as his dad jumps with him. An athlete will push herself to finish an Ironman triathlon if she's fueled by the cheers of her friends as she strives toward the finish line.

Take away the presence of others and these feats turn daunting. Childbirth, cliff diving, and endurance sports are different experiences when performed in isolation. The higher the risk and greater the struggle, the more we need to know we're not alone in it. Presence lends us courage to persist.

The same could be said for faith. It's easy to stay strong when life is good. We assume our comfort is proof of God's love. We sing songs, quote verses, fill gratitude journals, and preach rousing messages about the presence of God.

Until something happens that raises both the risk and the pain.

A diagnosis or a death. A child who wanders, a career that flounders, a church that fails. Poverty, chronic pain, injustice, unending loneliness. Political crisis, human atrocity, homelessness.

There is a suffering that pushes us beyond self-determination. No matter how we try to bootstrap our way to victory, we come up short. The trite cannot touch it; the untried cannot affect it. When we arrive in that place, agony makes us question God's reality. In the dark with our terrifying questions, our songs, quotes, and cliches don't hold up. God's silence seems to speak to His absence. We cry out in fear, "Where is God?"

Countries and governments, communities and families have been torn in two by differing answers to this question. It's a high-stakes conundrum, holding things like justice and meaning and purpose in its grip.

But what if God isn't absent in our struggle but fully present in it? And what if we could collect enough evidence of His presence to bring relief to our pain and anchor our faith outside the reach of it?

THE JORDAN RIVER

Hidden in the dusty pages of the Old Testament sits the story of a young leader named Joshua. An aid to the late Israelite deliverer Moses, Joshua found himself the new leader of God's people (Joshua 1). It was a daunting task to slip into Moses' enormous sandals and then to lead God's people to the promised land of Israel. Joshua needed help, and God gave it to him: "Moses my servant is dead. Now then, you and all these people, get ready to cross the Jordan River into the land I am about to give to them. . . . As I was with Moses, so I will be with you; I will never leave you nor forsake you" (Josh. 1:2, 5).

When Joshua needed courage, God promised Himself. Joshua didn't need more weapons or wisdom; he needed presence.

It's a good thing too. Because not long after setting out for the promised land, Joshua and the Israelites faced an impossible obstacle: the Jordan River. Running at flood stage, the waters were deep and turbulent, impossible to cross. But the promised land lay on the other side.

You can read the entire story in Joshua 3, but the short of it is this: God did something the Israelites would retell of for generations.

First, He told the Levite priests to carry the ark of the covenant into the middle of the Jordan. The moment their priestly toes touched the water, it piled up in a "heap" at a great distance (v. 16). Then, with dry ground spread out before them, God told the Israelites to cross safely to the other side.

All while the priests held the ark in the center.

We'll dig deeper into the implications of this story later. For now, it's enough to know that the ark represented God's presence. And that God's presence in the middle of the Jordan delivered His people in miraculous fashion. They danced, cheered, and slapped each other heartily on the back. They prayed for deliverance and God granted it.

Would ya look at that?! What a day!

God is good! He is with us!

But faith often lasts only as long as good fortune. Which is why God issued a final instruction to help anchor their faith when the rigors of life made them forget:

> When the whole nation had finished crossing the Jordan, the LORD said to Joshua, "Choose twelve men from among the people, one from each tribe, and tell them to take up twelve stones from the middle of the Jordan, from right where the priests are standing, and carry them over with you and put them down at the place where you stay tonight."
>
> So Joshua called together the twelve men he had appointed from the Israelites, one from each tribe, and said to them, "Go over before the ark of the LORD your God into the middle of the Jordan. Each of you is to take up a stone on his shoulder, according to the number of the tribes of the Israelites, to serve as a sign among you. In the future, when your children ask you, 'What do these stones mean?' tell them that the flow of the Jordan was cut off before the ark of the covenant of the LORD. When it crossed

> the Jordan, the waters of the Jordan were cut off. These stones are to be a memorial to the people of Israel forever." . . . And they are there to this day.
>
> —JOSHUA 4:1–7, 9

By divine miracle, the Israelites overcame the impossible. But God wasn't done. After they arrived on the other side of the Jordan, God sent twelve of them back to the river they'd just crossed to find twelve stones. Stones they wouldn't have seen without God's being in the middle of it. Stones that reminded them not only of their pain but of God's presence.

Then God told them to use those stones to build a marker. An altar.

Why? Because crossing the Jordan wasn't the end of their struggle.

This is my challenge to you as you walk through these pages. Hidden in the raging middle of your most harrowing experiences sit the makings of an altar, stones that bear evidence of God's presence and deliverance, even if it didn't look the way you thought it would. I want you to look for those stones. When you find them, I want you to pull them from the muck of your life and build a memorial.

These stones may be rocks from your back yard that you label accordingly. Or perhaps your stone is more experiential: a verse read, a note received, a gift given, a person encountered. The point is to identify moments when you experienced God's presence and then to mark them in such a way that you can return to them when life tempts you to forget.

Collect these twelve stones, one for each chapter, and set them up as a testimony. By the last page, you will have a twelve-stone memorial testifying to God's relentless presence with you.

THE INVITATION

In his poignant book *Soul Keeping*, pastor John Ortberg describes the paradoxical results of a pain-tried faith: "If you ask people who don't believe in God why they don't, the number one reason will be suffering. If you ask people who believe in God when they grew most spiritually, the number one answer will be suffering."[4]

During these long years of trauma, despair, and divine silence, I feared my faith was beyond resuscitation. But by a miracle of grace, what I thought would drown my faith is becoming the stones that give testimony to it. But it has required what Philip Yancey calls "a process of mining truth from [the] religious past."[5]

One day, you too will find yourself buried by questions you can't answer. It's a matter not of if but when. When that happens, you will need something more than what your understanding, competence, and power can give you.

You will need God Himself.

An altar of His presence that stands taller than the depths of your despair.

If you're already there, buried by crisis, you're safe here. My aim is not to deliver bandaid cliches and easy-to-swallow quotes. Nor will I preach theology from a pedestal to shame you for your shallow faith.

Relentless is a journey deep into the ugly archives of personal narrative and biblical history. It's you and me, backpack laden, together. Each of us gripping the hand of the other, embarking on an expedition into our complex stories and the gospel story, hoping to find God Himself standing in the middle of both. In the words of Yancey, "I [cling] fiercely to the stance of a pilgrim, for that is all I am. I have no religious sanction. I am neither pastor nor teacher, but an ordinary pilgrim, one person among many on a spiritual search. Unavoidably and by instinct, I question and reevaluate my faith all the time . . . Why am I still a Christian? What keeps me pursuing a gospel that has come to me amid so much distortion and static, that often sounds more like bad news than good?"[6]

These are the questions we will ask together. My greatest desire is that through these pages, we will encounter God's nearness.

Altars of His presence. The kind of proximity that has pursued us from the garden of Eden to the pages of Revelation. I pray that glimmers of Him surprise you, comfort you, and breathe new life into you. And I pray that the fact of His presence would so correct your faith of any theological misdirection that your darkest days—today or tomorrow—will be illuminated by His light.

You are never alone, my friend. Not even in dark basements where Death pounds on your door.

No, not even then.

His presence is relentless. Even when you can't reach for Him.

Especially then.

My life is my life—but naturally only as I saw it. Some might be just my perception of the event/experience. At the same time, I sincerely believe most of what I share is what really occurred or I wouldn't share it. . . .

I have worked hard all of my life to have "treasure-hunted" the painful events in my life that have shaped me. I have strived to find the nuggets of gold within the mountains of dross that composed my life's story.

—DAD, DECEMBER 8, 2011

CHAPTER 1

A Garden

A God Who Has Always Wanted to Be with You

Too many have never burst into the dazzling sunlight of God's conscious, manifest presence. Or if they perchance have, it is a rare experience and not a continuous delight.

—A. W. TOZER, *EXPERIENCING THE PRESENCE OF GOD*

Love by its nature seeks union.

—BRENNAN MANNING, *THE FURIOUS LONGING OF GOD*

It was my own secret garden, in the shade underneath our family's weeping willow tree.

Known for the fast growth of its "weeping" branches, my tree bent toward the ground like a hundred graceful arms honoring my presence. For a six-year-old girl, the willow provided retreat. It was my private hideaway, and within its falling branches I discovered the possibility of unwritten stories.

I spent hours in the willow's shade, a favorite book in hand or mind alight with dreams. Shutting the front door of our Tempe, Arizona, home behind me, I entered my tree with reverence, lowering my head and sweeping the branches to the side, stepping as if through a waterfall behind which I'd discover a new world. An adventure awaited.

Hidden in my leafy cathedral, I became more than an insecure six-year-old girl. I was a mother cooking supper for her husband and small children. A teacher leading her classroom through the finer points of math and art. Or if the day was particularly perfect, I became Laura Ingalls Wilder, embracing adventure in the untamed West.

Other days, I settled underneath my canopy without a need to do anything. Sheltered from the sun, I lay on my back on the dry desert earth, eyes up to the sky. By myself, but not alone.

God was with me. I did not question it. Although fireworks didn't light up the sky, nor did I experience the rumbling of a godlike voice, I believed in the miracle of divine presence. I could hear Him in the sound of birdsong, see Him in the rustling of the leaves, feel Him in the warmth of the morning sun.

I'm with you, My girl.

As I sit in my office in Denver nearly one thousand miles from Tempe, I feel a thousand years removed from that innocence under the willow tree. Although four decades separate the woman from the girl, the distance my faith has traveled feels much farther. My once untried belief now wears thin.

Reformed theologian John Calvin writes, "Without knowledge of self there is no knowledge of God."[7] Just as the brushstrokes of a painting tell us something of the artist who conceived it, finding meaning in our suffering requires a careful search through our stories and a mining for glimmers of the God who authored them or allowed them.

Even so, it's always a risk to travel back in time and recreate circumstances from fading memories. Forty years is a long time to forget. And no doubt I have forgotten quite a bit.

When it comes to the journey of faith, sometimes ascertaining how we arrived at this *X* on the spot isn't so much about recalling precise memories as it is about recognizing how those memories precisely marked us. How the experiences and relationships, losses and gains made us *feel*. And then how those feelings impressed us, molded us, and changed what we believed to be true. Where I lack precision, I hope to add discernment to understand how, over time, circumstances weathered the faith I see in the brushstrokes of memory.

Like the willow tree's branches, these bowing arms give honor to both a little girl's certainty of God's presence and the grown woman's wrestling with it. And to how, years removed from the innocence of the willow tree, she feared she'd lost her faith.

Five years before the willow tree, my parents walked down a church aisle and chose Jesus. This is where my faith journey begins, because their faith became my own. And it changed everything for all of us.

Although church attendance was part of my parents' childhood, faith wasn't. (There is a difference, you know.) My maternal grandmother took my mom to church once or twice a month. Dad, on the other hand, went to church nearly every week. His stepmother was the organist and pianist, so he regularly joined her. Don't let his stellar attendance fool you, though. As Dad told it, his weekly churching had little to do with any deep faith. "I went for the girls," he said with a wink.

But that all changed after my twentysomething Dad spent two years in the United States Army and a faith-testing place called Vietnam.

Dad was twenty-four years old and newly married when he enlisted in the army. The date was September 11, 1968. He later told me he didn't want to wait for the draft, that he wanted service to be his choice, not his obligation. I suppose this allowed him a measure of control after an out-of-control childhood.

So after only thirty-one days of marriage, Dad joined the army during a time of war.

After basic military training in Fort Leonard Wood, Missouri, and field artillery school training in Fort Sill, Oklahoma, Dad shipped out to Phu Loi, Vietnam. The date was September 10, 1969, one day after Mom and Dad spent their first night together in their new home. He wouldn't see her face or their home again for nearly a year.

It's hard to imagine the man I knew, the one who seemed so hard and unyielding, as the boy who stepped out of a plane into the mess that was Vietnam. I think of my own boys, the oldest two of whom are now older than he was, and try to imagine it, both those who left and the families who sent them. No one yet knew that the jungle would take the best of them, even if they managed to get back home.

Years later, Dad shared bits and pieces of those two hard years. He told me how, within days of his arrival and while on guard duty, incoming artillery fire caught him unaware and he found himself diving for a foxhole in terror. He learned quickly always to stay alert. He told me about the heavy artillery units and the radar artillery devices he worked with, the ones that left him with a lifetime of hearing loss. Even so, there were times when I worked alongside him in the back yard and his head would pop up.

"A chopper's coming," he'd tell me.

I thought he was crazy; I couldn't hear a thing. But every time, within seconds, a helicopter came into view to prove him right.

He told me about the terrible food and how hard it was to be away from his new wife—the quiet and shy woman who one day became my mother. With a smile, he'd recall how she sent care packages filled with cookies and canned Mexican food that he devoured like a starving man. Then he'd tell me how he read and reread her letters, a lifeline in the days before cell phones and the internet. His favorite story? The two times my mom "called" with the help of a local ham radio operator near her home in Arizona. The sound of her voice kept him hanging on.

But what I most remember about Dad's retelling of his Vietnam years was the pain he endured when he came back home. Those were the stories Dad told again and again, how strangers spit at him when he climbed off the plane and hurled insults and trash as he searched for Mom's face in the airport crowd. Many of those who claimed to be his friends before he left disappeared when he came home. Until he hid his uniform and grew out his hair, those who saw him punished him.

As if he hadn't already endured enough trauma.

Besides Mom, Dad's one light during those dark days was the promise of his grandparents' prayers. Devout Baptists, they'd always told him they prayed for him. When he crossed oceans and continents to fight in an impossible war, he took the reassurance of his grandparents' words with him.

This memory served him well when one day he found himself in the middle of an ambush.

As best as I can remember it, Dad said the enemy fire hit unexpectedly. Three companies of soldiers were on the move, Dad's truck situated in between the other two. Out of nowhere, fire erupted from the bush. Everything happened fast. All Dad knew was that the truck in front of him erupted, as did the one behind him. But his truck and team remained untouched.

He later told me he thought of his grandmother's prayers in that moment. And although he didn't yet know God, he believed he'd been spared for a reason. The experience marked him, and it drove him when he finally got home.

A little more than a year later, after Dad had returned to the States and his wife, a coworker by the name of Dave Mostek invited him to church. I'm not sure why he accepted. Maybe it was the lingering nightmares of Vietnam and the fact of his grandmother's prayers. Maybe it was his memories of an abusive and chaotic childhood. Or perhaps it was out of commitment to his new family.

Regardless, Dad went. Choice, not obligation. Searching for meaning in the life he had yet to make sense of. A few months later, after devouring the Bible and trying to understand this God who claimed to love him, Dad and Mom were baptized. December 10, 1971. A little more than four months after I was born.

And with that public declaration, Dad became a devoted—and desperate—disciple of this Jesus he hoped would save him.

⋄

At the beginning of time, before the world was divided into dark and light, earth and sea, fish and mammal, man and woman, *God was.* This is what I was taught. And this is what I've long believed.

"In the beginning God created," Genesis 1:1 says. But the rest of the first chapter explains the means of that creation.

"And God said, 'Let there be light,' and there was light" (v. 3).

"And God said, 'Let there be a vault between the waters to separate water from water'" (v. 6).

"And God said, 'Let the land produce living creatures'" (v. 24).

And then, as if He hadn't already said enough, the creator makes His final pronouncement in His final act of creating.

"Then God said, 'Let us make mankind in our image, in our likeness'" (v. 26).

And God said.

At the beginning of your story and mine sit those same three words. We forget this as we argue about our differences and assume our staunch positions on politics and religion and complex issues and events. We seem to think we are so different from each other. And yet at the core of each person's creation sits one unifying impetus.

God's words.

According to the biblical narrative, that means each one of us—male, female, married, single, Republican, Democrat, black, white, Asian, Latino, blue collar, white collar—found our first breath as a result of these three words.

And God said.

God created, "creates" even still, by speaking. The power of His voice weaves the fabric of life. This is not new for those of us who hold faith as part of our substance.

My question is, "Why?"

Why words? Why did God create with words? He could have started our stories with a magic wand. Or a laser light show. Or the blink of an eye. Or a killer John Travolta dance move.

Or, as would be my preference, the Wonder Twins' rings.

"Wonder Twin powers, activate!"

Seriously, hands down, the best creation narrative ever.

Alas, rather than light shows, dance moves, or Wonder Twin rings, the creator chose to create with words.

"The earth was formless and empty, darkness was over the surface of the deep, and the Spirit of God was hovering over the waters. *And God said* . . ." (Gen. 1:2–3).

Words piercing the darkness with light. Words providing a harbor of land in the middle of the seas. Words throwing lights up into the sky and vegetation on the ground.

It was that simple. God spoke. Darkness rolled back, light came, and with it, *life*. My life. And yours.

From the first day and night, words were the means of connection. Words brought God's desire to fruition, connecting His heart with ours, and ours with each other's. Because of divine word, our hearts beat, our brains think, and our lungs fill with air.

Then, in response to God's word-driven creation, creation itself responded with words. David says it this way in Psalm 19:

> The heavens declare the glory of God;
> the skies proclaim the work of his hands.
> Day after day they pour forth speech;
> night after night they reveal knowledge.
> They have no speech, they use no words;
> no sound is heard from them.

> Yet their voice goes out into all the earth,
> their words to the ends of the world.
>
> —VERSES 1–4

God speaks. Life begins. Then life turns around and testifies to the one who spoke first.

This reciprocity is key to vibrant relationship. It's what distinguishes humans from animals, the way we receive words and then respond to them. The way we process, relate to, and interact with one another through words. Like the intersection of two busy streets, words bring people going in different directions to the same point on the map.

"Nice to meet you!"

"Will you marry me?"

"It's a girl!"

And, "I'll take a large, thin crust with pepperoni, olives, banana peppers, and extra cheese."

But just as words give life, words also steal life. Each one of us could recount too many instances when words wounded, interrupting relationship with irreparable pain.

"I'm disappointed in you."

"I'm leaving you."

"You have six months to live."

Which is why, in the middle of God's speaking and creating and celebrating, Evil used words to wound the source of all relationship.

"Now the serpent was more crafty than any of the wild animals the Lord God had made. He said to the woman, 'Did God really say . . .'" (Gen. 3:1).

Satan's first tactic? Stir up doubt around God's words.

"The woman said to the serpent, 'We may eat fruit from the trees in the garden, but God did say . . .'" (vv. 2–3).

The woman starts out strong, leaning into the strength of God's words, remembering hardcore truth in the face of slippery doubt. But it doesn't last.

"'You will not certainly die,' the serpent said to the woman. 'For God knows that when you eat from it your eyes will be opened, and you will be like God, knowing good and evil'" (vv. 4–5).

When you and I open our eyes first thing in the morning, light enters. Closed eyes deliver dark, and open eyes deliver light.

But in this case, the opposite happened. The moment Adam and Eve made a decision from a place of doubt, their eyes opened and a darkness descended they would never be able to shake. As if a veil was lowered over God's presence, Adam and Eve experienced an immediate and eclipsing despair.

A separation.

Just as God's words inaugurated life, Satan's words initiated death. Light interrupted by darkness. Relationship severed by distrust.

In the beginning, words cemented relationship, binding us to the author of words and other word-loving creations. Words assured us we would never be alone.

Only it didn't work out that way. Adam and Eve's response—and now ours—to the question, "Did God really say?" created a break in relationship we'd never be able to bridge.

Although words joined us, words, in the end, separated us.

And we've been aching to restore that relationship ever since.

Before doubt interrupted the divine-human relationship, Adam and Eve lived drunk on intimacy, intoxicated with loving and being loved.

Eden was their haven, a holy sanctum where the creator walked with the created. God cared for their every need—emotional, physical, spiritual. They had no concept of words like loneliness, isolation, hunger, pain, neglect, abuse, and abandonment. No one suffered from insecurity or codependency. God's presence filled the space around them and in them with the warmth of His nearness.

But then a snake enticed them with the thought of something more. And that thought became the slightest seed of dissatisfaction in a perfectly satisfying existence.

Rather than savor what they already had—God Himself—they longed for what they lacked—to *be* God. They exchanged the guarantee of intimacy for the lust for supremacy. They gambled it all and ended up with nothing. Greed broke their God bond, creating a divide so wide, long, high, and deep they could do nothing to bridge it. No matter their regret, they could not undo what had been done.

Which is why their impulse was to cover up and hide. In response to their shame, God made Adam and Eve animal-skin clothing to cover up the nakedness that now made them feel insecure and exposed. But to make leather dresses and dress shirts, an animal needed to die.

One life for another. Innocence to erase guilt.

Problem is, Adam and Eve soon learned it would take more than an animal skin to bring absolution. Their betrayal had caused a trauma—emotional, physical, spiritual. No matter how many nights they spent regretting what they'd done, the impact of this separation followed them out of their perfect garden and into their messy, complicated everyday lives.

And their aching loneliness without a close Father proved the most painful punishment of all.

This same aching loneliness isolated me in the basement during those dark days postcancer. I longed for a present and protecting Father. But suffering shone a dark spotlight on the human condition. In the grip of pain and trauma, I faced mortality and felt afresh the chasm between God and humankind.

It was a loneliness I could not relieve. And it felt an awful lot like abandonment.

Of course, no one locked the basement door and forced me into isolation. My family reassured me of their love. But suffering created a separation, a wall between my reality and theirs. I couldn't act as if nothing had happened, as if I hadn't changed. I could not dress up in a pretty faith and pretend that my existence hadn't been shattered. So I hid in the dark, where my external environment resembled my internal one.

God turned silent. My friends and family felt distant. What was left to live for?

Although my days hiding in the basement lasted less than a week, the shroud of otherness and despair followed me for years. When I finally climbed the stairs and reentered day-to-day life with my family, the feeling of being cut off went with me. I tried to love my husband and mother my children. I continued to read my Bible and attend church. But the efforts felt empty, devoid of life.

You and I were made for garden living: daily, intimate connection with God and others, where every need is met through the sweet sufficiency of authentic relationship.

But Eden marked a break in relationship, a break the Bible calls sin. And although sin didn't cause cancer, my suffering served as a painful reminder of how far we've all traveled from the safety of garden living.

We all live outside Eden's gates, hands gripping the iron and hearts longing to return to the place our souls remember. Although we can limp along self-sufficiently and independently for a time, sooner or later life serves up a circumstance we can't muscle our way through. When that happens, we feel the sting of our separated existence.

"When Jesus is near, all is well and nothing seems difficult," Thomas á Kempis, a fifteenth-century priest, writes. "When He is absent, all is hard. When Jesus does not speak within, all other comfort is empty, but if He says only a word, it brings great consolation."[8]

I needed a word, a message from God Himself. A reminder that His presence was with me, in spite of the pain.

Whether He didn't give it or I didn't hear it, the only thing I heard for a long time was silence.

ALTAR STONE 1

LOOKING FOR GOD'S PRESENCE IN THE BEGINNING OF YOUR STORY

The willow tree is one of my earliest memories of experiencing God. The branches provided safety, imagination, and possibility. It was a haven of sorts, one I needed. Think back to your earliest memories. Whether they are good or bad, I believe God provided glimmers of Himself there. Consider your earliest inklings of a greater goodness before adulthood and the unexpected life clouded innocent belief. Can you see hints of your Father? Can you see evidence of His desire to be with you? The Bible says that when you were still in your mother's womb, God knew you, loved you, weaved the cells and synapses of your body together into a glorious work of art (Psalm 139). You were not invisible to Him even then. Pray for God to open your eyes to see what you may have missed. Then write it down. Mark it. This is your first altar stone.

My childhood is dominated by cloudy events, painful uncertainty, and dishevel . . . I was born in the four-pound range and that is how I gained the nickname of "Punky" . . . My mom liked to dress me like a little girl, which early on caused me to be teased by family members and others . . . I remember I was having a birthday party [and] I guess I was "acting silly like a girl," so she took me inside and dressed me like a little girl and sent me outside to play with my friends. They made fun of me to the point that I ran to my room crying and wouldn't come back out. I only remember having one other birthday party . . .

[My] parents divorced sometime in the first grade . . . I was a "sickly" kid—that is why I flunked first grade . . . our house was in quarantine most of that year, with me having multiple cases of scarlatina, chicken pox, pneumonia, and a number of different kinds of measles. There were days when my mom would let me sit on our front porch to get fresh air . . . and I would wonder where the people were going and [if they] were happy.

—**DAD, DECEMBER 8, 2011**

CHAPTER 2

A Smoking Firepot and a Blazing Torch

A GOD WHO PROMISES TO BE WITH YOU

> Steadfastness in believing doth not exclude all temptations from without. When we say a tree is firmly rooted, we do not say the wind never blows upon it. The house that is built on the rock, is not free from assaults and storms.
>
> —JOHN OWEN, *THE STRENGTH OF FAITH*

I arrived one year after my dad came back from Vietnam. July 31, 1971.

Funny how that works.

After receiving leave from the army to return stateside to work on his master's degree, Dad and Mom moved to Orange, California, where he got a job at State Farm Insurance. Simultaneously, I am told, he pursued a "fatherhood degree."

Awkward.

Nine months later, my seven-pound, dark-eyed, pink-cheeked, and perfectly bald self entered the world.

Earlier that same year, on February 9, 1971, another force rocked California. While sleeping in bed next to my dad, my pregnant mother woke up to a jolt. Thinking my father was shaking the bed in his sleep, she rolled over to tell him to knock it off. And that's when she realized the earthshaking movement wasn't Dad's fault.

At 6:00 a.m. on an ordinary Tuesday, the San Fernando Earthquake—also known as the Sylmar Earthquake—rocked the San Fernando Valley just north of Los Angeles, leaving buildings and lives turned upside down. By the time the earth settled, sixty-four people lay dead and more than 2,500 were injured. Perhaps the most affected was the San Fernando Veterans Administration Hospital in Sylmar. Built in 1926, it didn't have the supports to help it withstand a violent shaking. It collapsed in on itself during those twelve predawn seconds, killing more than forty people, including some of my dad's fellow veterans.[9]

Thankfully, Mom and Dad lived far enough away to suffer only mild rumblings of the 6.6 magnitude quake. Still, Mom told me that story for years, how her pregnant self was thoroughly irritated with Dad for waking her up with his tossing and turning. And I liked the bragging rights of having endured a massive earthquake, even if I did so in an amniotic bathtub.

Although I haven't experienced an earthquake since, it was not the last time something rocked my world.

Like all newborns, the baby girl born to those two loving and committed parents held nothing but trust for them. She didn't understand that the twenty-seven-year-old man who refused to hold her was doing his best to piece himself together from the crushing of a hard childhood and a controversial war. She knew nothing of child abuse and PTSD, how the rumbling of a distant earthquake could stir up fight-or-flight responses. And how these unseen forces could cause him to erupt without warning, like land mines in lush green stretches of jungle.

She didn't understand how surviving a war—in childhood and adulthood—changes a person. She simply loved him with the blind affection a little girl feels for her daddy.

But trauma doesn't discriminate between adults and

tenderhearted girls. I adored my father. And I also grew up terrified of him.

My father was a man of contradictions, a man of such knotted complexity that I couldn't unravel the mystery of him until years after he was gone. What I know about those early years are collected from reconstructed memories and his occasional, painful recollections shared in short emotional bursts over the years. I believe Dad revealed those details because he desperately wanted me to understand him, to know why, especially in those years of my childhood, he behaved the way he did.

Undeniably, Dad was a good man, an honest provider, a hungry spiritual seeker. He read his Bible, went to church, always kept his promises, told the truth.

But he could also be rigid, critical, and capable of explosive anger and verbal tirades that turned his face red and his eyes to fire. I never knew when it would come, when a dinner plate left on the counter, a trash can left on the curb, or a bedroom left untidy would trigger a land mine and cause his wrath to rain down. I learned early to be on my guard, to watch every nuance of facial expression and body language. And I especially learned the critical importance of doing what I was told.

As a result, my childhood became its own sort of tricky battleground, one moment a lush haven and the next a fear-riddled war zone. I tried desperately to avoid stepping on anything that would set Dad off. At the same time, I chased after him with the instinct of a girl hungry for her father's love.

So the trauma of his childhood and Vietnam became my own. This is what happens, of course. Trauma doesn't produce only one perpetrator and one victim. Instead, the blame can be cast back for generations, each wounded child becoming an adult who never wanted to cause similar pain, and yet seemed helpless to stop the cycle of relational disconnect they inherited.

A little girl—or a little boy—doesn't know how to unravel this kind of knotted familial complexity, how to stop it before it replicates and continues. Instead, she sees the world in terms of cause and effect. She believes she is somehow to blame for her pain, that it is her "badness" that caused the conflict. Whether consciously or not, she believes that if she does everything right, she can keep her world from going wrong.

In the innocent eyes of a little girl, good behavior means love. So pleasing my father became my only recourse to being close to him. And since duty spoke the language he best understood, I worked like a loyal soldier, day after day, trying to be good enough to be loved.

I became a Christian as a result of an early childhood addiction to communion wafers.

I may be overstating it, but the fact that the extraordinarily long Sunday church services came with a snack definitely added incentive. And according to my parents, I couldn't take communion until I chose to follow Jesus and was baptized. So this is how it went down.

It was two months before my seventh birthday when my family left Tempe, Arizona. Recently I learned that Arizona's state motto is *Ditat Deus*, which means "God enriches." In hindsight, I find it quite appropriate considering that Arizona was the place where my parents' early faith was tended and nurtured. And it was also the location where I first learned the basics about Christianity.

Even so, my clearest memory of our Arizona church experience isn't of a Bible story or a beloved Sunday school teacher, as lovely as that would sound. Instead, it's the Fourth of July service when my little brother jammed the plastic handheld United States flag up his nose and broke the plastic tip off in his sinus cavity.

Land of the free, indeed.

Needless to say, our patriotism (and faith) found expression in the emergency room that year.

Apparently, God enriches *and* extracts. Glory.

Mom and Dad had both been raised in Arizona, Mom in Phoenix and Dad in Globe-Miami, a mountain town known for its mines, including the Inspiration Copper Mine. Dad, his grandfather, and his great-grandfather all worked that mine at some point in their lives. The Grand Canyon state was their home and history, housing the vast majority of their relatives and memories. But when Dad was offered a promotion and transfer with a national insurance company, they packed up my brother and me and headed east to the "Land of Lincoln."

Normal, Illinois, to be precise.

(Yes, *Normal*. Go ahead. Make your lame joke. I've already heard them all.)

The first Sunday after our U-Haul pulled into town, we showed up in church. And within weeks, Mom and Dad started serving in some capacity. For nearly two decades we stayed at that church, and in all that time I can count on a single hand the number of Sundays (and Sunday nights and Wednesdays) we failed to cross the threshold. Eventually, Dad became an elder, Mom a secretary and registrar for the church preschool. But before all that, they spent Saturdays prepping Sunday's communion trays, among other things. And while my parents filled hundreds of tiny plastic cups with a plastic squeeze bottle of grape juice, my brother and I stole communion wafers from the finished trays.

I like to think my extra ingestion of Jesus' body and blood provided an additional covering of forgiveness for my excessive communion-cracker sins.

It wasn't just my hunger for Saturday morning snacks that drew me to the Christian faith. Every Sunday, I sat next to my father in the second pew from the front, right side, near the center aisle. When we stood, I heard his enthusiastic baritone belt out songs like

"I'll Fly Away" and hymns like "Great Is Thy Faithfulness." When we sat down in our wooden pew and the minister began his sermon, I watched Dad's angled lefthanded scrawl record copious notes of everything he was learning.

Dad was a man who grew up in the dark and finally discovered light. Faith gave him what he longed for—structure, safety, and belonging. And I longed for him. So with my white leather King James Bible in hand, I took my own notes, copying every word he wrote, verbatim. I may not have understood a lick of it, but soon I loved church too. With or without the communion wafers.

"I want to be baptized," I told them a few months later. Within the week, the minister showed up at our front door, and my parents led him to our formal living room and the flowered 1970s sofa, the sofa we never sat on. Apparently, baptism came with additional perks.

I still remember how nervous I felt. And the minister's four questions:

"Who do you think God is?"

I must've answered with acceptable grade-school accuracy, because he moved on to question two. *Whew.*

"Okay, and who is Jesus? Why did He come, and what did He do?"

I had this one in the bag. I knew a lot about Jesus. He was the guy who died on the cross. Again, I must've wowed him with my spiritual insight, because he launched the doozy of all faith questions.

"Now, this question is more difficult."

I nodded with all the seriousness of a founding father signing the Declaration of Independence.

"Who is the Holy Spirit? And what does He do?"

Uh-oh.

I was stumped. The Holy Spirit was an enigma to me. I didn't get it, couldn't wrap my little brain around the idea of a spirit-God-thing that was separate from God, but also God. I must've mumbled something that didn't sound entirely heretical, and he let my innocent ignorance pass with a kind smile.

"That one's tough for a lot of grownups too."

Glory hallelujah, I passed. He wrapped up the conversation with one final question.

"Why do you want to follow Jesus?"

"Because I love Him."

Honestly, I wanted to *be* loved. And from what I could tell, being baptized was like putting God on the hook. He couldn't get rid of me once I did the big dunk. I was too young to recognize the sliver of a lie hidden in the belief.

God didn't need my baptism to be hooked on me.

A week or two later, on Sunday, October 29, 1978, I sat next to my mom and dad in the second pew from the front, right side, near the center aisle. We sang a handful of hymns. The minister preached a sermon. My dad took notes, and I'm sure I copied every word.

Then when the minister started his closing comments, my heart accelerated. He directed us to our hymnals, told us to turn to something like "Just As I Am" or "Softly and Tenderly." Then he said words that I knew were for me.

"If anyone here would like to accept Jesus' invitation to follow Him, now is the time. He's waiting. Will you come?"

The organist started her music and, in unison, the congregants rose, hymnals in hand, and prepared to sing.

My heart pounded so loudly I could hardly hear the music. I tugged on Dad's arm.

"Will you please come with me?" The walk to the front looked so very long. I didn't want to do it alone.

He shook his head, unyielding. "No, Michele. This is your decision. You need to do it alone."

I could feel the tears welling, the fear leaking out my eyes. I didn't want to do it alone. But I knew better than to defy my father.

With a deep breath and determination, my seven-year-old self squeezed out from the pew and made her way down the center aisle toward the front.

Jesus was worth it. With or without the communion crackers.

⸻

When Adam and Eve broke the one rule God said they couldn't break, they lost more than their garden. They lost closeness with God Himself. After living intoxicated with intimacy, they now suffered the hangover of separation.

But Adam and Eve's trauma didn't end with them. It never does. Instead, it impacted the God-human bond for every boy and girl born after them. Eden's memory may have died with Adam and Eve, but the longing for gardenlike intimacy with God and each other passed from generation to generation like a disease, infiltrating human DNA and our resulting relationships ever since.

We get a small taste of this generational trauma in the first eleven chapters of Genesis, where we read the ugly details of the children and grandchildren who followed Adam and Eve, including stories like Cain and Abel, Noah and the flood, and the tower of Babel. Immorality and increasing familial conflict in abundance. The wrecking of the divine-human relationship wasn't temporary. It polluted our experience of relationships on every front, creating discord and murder where before there was peace and love.

While it's easy to imagine how Eden's banishment affected humanity, I rarely consider how the disaster must've wounded God's heart. From His first word in Genesis 1, God created us to be connected to Him, enjoying daily communion and companionship.

This was His great desire. But we—His beloved—pushed Him away. Tempted by greener grass and our own power, we rebelled, packed our bags, and drove away.

To a God whose nature is love (1 John 4:8), our rejection cut

Him to His core. A relationship torn in two doesn't wound just one party. So, rent by pain and driven by love, God determined to repair the relationship, beginning with one man named Abram.

> "I will make you into a great nation,
> and I will bless you;
> I will make your name great,
> and you will be a blessing.
> I will bless those who bless you,
> and whoever curses you I will curse;
> and all peoples on earth
> will be blessed through you."
>
> —GENESIS 12:2–3

"I will bless you," God said. "All peoples on earth will be blessed through you."

In a world marked by trauma and dysfunction, God promised healing through relationship.

A counselor once told me that wounds created in relationship can be healed only in relationship. God knew this. So He set out to heal the relational distance beginning with one man and promised healing to the rest of us through him.

The problem, however, was that Abram—later known as Abraham—and his wife, Sarah, didn't have any children. It's tough to bless subsequent generations when the first one hasn't even started. To begin, God sends them to Canaan, a land He later promises to give Abram and all his descendants. After setting up house near the hills of Bethel of Canaan, Abram builds an altar to God "and called on the name of the Lord" (v. 8).

Still no baby. Years passed, decades even. And Abram questioned both his mental health and God's promise. Either he'd misunderstood or he'd imagined the whole thing. Centenarians typically don't send out birth announcements.

This is why God and Abram sat down for another powwow in Genesis 15:

> After this, the word of the LORD came to Abram in a vision:
>
> "Do not be afraid, Abram.
> I am your shield,
> your very great reward."
>
> But Abram said, "Sovereign LORD, what can you give me since I remain childless and . . . a servant in my household will be my heir."
>
> Then the word of the LORD came to him: "This man will not be your heir, but a son who is your own flesh and blood will be your heir." He took him outside and said, "Look up at the sky and count the stars—if indeed you can count them." Then he said to him, "So shall your offspring be."
>
> —VERSES 1–5

One more time, God reassures Abram of His promise and His provision. But this time, God offers more than words. He serves up something called covenant.

By definition, a covenant is "an agreement between two or more parties outlining mutual rights and responsibilities."[10] The most common Old Testament (Hebrew) word for covenant is *berit*, which can mean "agreement" or "arrangement." It may come from the root *bara*, which means "to eat bread with," signifying the common sharing of a meal during the covenant ceremony.

The first covenant was cut in the garden of Eden, when God killed animals to create leather skins to cover Adam and Eve's nakedness and sin. This is known as the Edenic Covenant. Then, for hundreds of years following the Eden banishment, animal sacrifice became the metaphor for broken relationship and the cost of securing it.

To those of us who grew up in the age of PETA, the practice sounds archaic and inhumane. But in ancient civilizations, animals and livestock represented income and status. To sacrifice an animal or to offer it in pledge was to make a payment or enforce an agreement. Contracts were sealed in blood, just as your signature binds you to a mortgage or a car contract. In the case of covenant, animals were cut in two and both parties walked through the pieces, in a sense saying, "This is what you can do to me if I fail to keep my promise." The ceremony complete, both parties were now bound to their end of the agreement upon penalty of death.

Starting in Genesis 15:9, God gives Abraham a set of covenant-cutting instructions. "Bring me a heifer, a goat and a ram, each three years old, along with a dove and a young pigeon." After gathering the animals, Abraham cuts the heifer, goat, and ram in half as instructed, and arranges the pieces across from each other, creating an aisle down the center. This is a ceremony with which Abram would've been familiar. He'd recognize it as the making of an agreement, one that would be sealed by both parties walking through blood.

"As the sun was setting, Abram fell into a deep sleep, and a thick and dreadful darkness came over him" (v. 12).

God speaks in the darkness. And what happens next rattles both heaven and earth with its implications: "When the sun had set and darkness had fallen, a smoking firepot with a blazing torch appeared and passed between the pieces. On that day the LORD made a covenant with Abram" (vv. 17–18).

The animals are killed, the table set, the covenant ready to be sealed. But there is one significant difference in the ceremony that certainly shocked the sandals right off of Abraham's feet.

Only God walks through the pieces.

In this blood-sealing covenant agreement between God and humankind, God states the terms: He will be their God, and they will be His people. But the only person on the hook to hold up their agreement is God Himself. In a sense, God says, "This is what you can do to Me if I fail to keep My promise. Moreover, this is what you can do to Me if *you* fail to keep your promise."

Whereas a contract is all about protecting the self, divine covenant protects *the relationship.* Covenant isn't a transaction; it's *an attaching* of two parties. As one commentary states, covenant is less a contract or a promise and more a "binding pledge," one that cannot be breached or broken.[11] But ultimately God knew it was a pledge we wouldn't—couldn't—keep. So, out of devotion to a dying people, God alone walked down the aisle, leaving His seat of divine distance to enter a binding relationship with us.

Although I may have been seven years old when I walked down a church aisle to show God how much I loved Him, God's love walked down an aisle for me long before.

His is the First Love. The resolute, relentless love that promises to heal us from our traumas. His love bridged the divide and determined to restore the relationship long before you and I knew we needed Him to do that. And for reasons we can't possibly comprehend, God put Himself alone on the hook for the keeping of the promise.

From Eden until today, humankind has lived marked by the wounds and wars that changed us. We see evidence in the abundance of broken families, abused children, struggling churches, and the ever-growing epidemic of addictions and diseases. We see it in the day's breaking news, coffee shop conversations, and social media rants. This isn't the way it's supposed to be, and we know it.

Of course, when we're not blaming someone else, we work hard to heal ourselves. We read books, take medication, find counselors, eat healthy, practice yoga, join a gym, attend church, vote. We learn, we grow, we mature, and we keep trying.

But in spite of our best efforts, we know there must be something more than the patched-up, complex lives we cling to. We can feel it in our bones. We need an all-out rescue, one we can't orchestrate or effect.

We have it. And it started with a covenant cut in an ancient ceremony binding God to us at the cost of His own blood.

A covenant promise that cost God everything He had and, in the process, gave us everything we lack.

ALTAR STONE 2

LOOKING FOR GOD'S PRESENCE IN HIS PROMISES

It's far easier to remember the broken promises than the kept ones. Without much effort, I can recall a fairly lengthy list of prayers God didn't answer like I expected Him to. And often, I equate an unanswered request as evidence of a promise unkept. Recently, my preteen daughter asked to do something that I felt wasn't appropriate for her age or maturity. I told her no. Naturally, she retaliated by letting me know how I was failing as a mother. She interpreted my no as a breach in my commitment to be a good mother to her. The truth, however, is that I was following through on my promise to love her, teach her, and keep her safe. But she couldn't see that from her eleven-year-old vantage point. Now that you have the position of adulthood, look back on your youth. Although you may have had moments when it seemed as if God failed you, how did He keep His promise to love and protect you? Can you see evidence of His love for you? Pray for God to open your eyes to see what you have missed. Then write it down. Mark it. This is your second altar stone.

What I remember in the early years was spending time with my grandpa and grandma . . . These are very sweet memories . . . I always felt loved by them. I played checkers with Grandpa and listened to the radio. Later on, we'd watch the ball games on TV. I would work puzzles with Grandma and would help her in the kitchen. I remember that on the days that Grandpa would work, he'd walk "up the hill" to the [Inspiration Copper Mine], located outside the backyard gate of their home. Then, at the end of the day, I would wait by the back gate to watch him walk down the hill. Grandma would always have his hot dinner ready and on the table waiting for him. We'd pray and then eat. Afterwards, we'd often sit on the front porch and visit or go to the side yard and sit in the swing.

It was only after I met and married [your mom] that my grandma told [her] that my mom or my dad would drop me off at their doorstep when they were going on a [partying binge]—sometimes for days.

—DAD, DECEMBER 8, 2011

CHAPTER 3

A Ladder and a Limp

A GOD WHO MEETS YOU WHERE YOU ARE

Ultimately, mourning means facing what wounds us in the presence of One who can heal.

—HENRI J. M. NOUWEN, *TURN MY MOURNING INTO DANCING*

There was no excuse. I was wrong. Even at eight years old, I knew better.

I stared at my bedroom ceiling through the dark, my purple Holly Hobbie bedspread pulled straight and taut under my chin. Memories of what I'd done plagued me.

Earlier that evening, I'd huddled in my room while my angry father punished my six-year-old brother for some childhood misdemeanor. Although I knew he deserved it—and felt the slightest twinge of satisfaction at his misery—I listened to his punishment as if it were my own.

I knew what it felt like to be the recipient of Dad's displeasure. And I knew I deserved his anger just as my brother did.

But Dad didn't yet know what I'd done.

It had started earlier that afternoon in my third-grade classroom when other kids passed notes behind Ms. Rankin's back. While she wrote her lesson in a chalky haze on the blackboard, my peers sent small folded squares of lined notebook paper back and forth.

Eventually one landed on my desk, my name written in third-grade script on the outside. And although I knew we weren't allowed to pass notes in class, my curiosity got the best of me. I slid it into my lap, out of the eyesight of the teacher, and unfolded the square to read its message.

Whatever the note said wasn't kind. Within moments I'd penciled an equally hurtful reply, full of hot anger and foul language. Although I can't remember the sender's message, I have no trouble recalling my potent retort: "I hope you pee your pants."

As I said, foul language. Of the third-grade variety. Not my proudest moment.

Hot as a hornet bent on inflicting pain, I folded the note up and passed it back the way it had come. I no longer remember the recipient or why she had me fired up. But I'll never forget what happened next.

The teacher looked up just as my wicked words passed from one hand to the next.

"I'll take that," she demanded, abandoning the chalkboard and reaching for the folded white square of paper carrying my penciled improprieties.

Instantly, my anger melted into mortification. I'd been caught. *My* note. *My* handwriting. *My* name.

With a flick of her wrist, she grabbed the note out of my classmate's hand, unfolded it, and read it.

Every rotten word.

Then, without comment, she carried it back to her desk and placed it front and center, where the entire class—and I—could see it glowing like white-hot fire.

I'm pretty sure all color drained from my face. I stared at the condemning evidence holding vigil on her desk, certain I was about to die a thousand deaths at the hand of my teacher. Worse, if any pieces of me remained by the end of the day, I'd be sent home, where Dad would finish me off. This is what terrified me most of all.

Ms. Rankin never said a word, which made my suffering worse. It was, perhaps, the longest afternoon of my life. Finally, when the bell signaled a break for recess, I stayed behind while my friends went out to play. I needed to get the note back.

When the last third grader left the classroom, I shuffled toward my teacher's desk. Embarrassed and out of my mind with fear, I burst into tears the moment she looked me in the eye, blubbering words like "I'm sorry" and "I'll never do it again." With excessive penitence and obvious remorse, I begged her to let me have the note. I thought if I could destroy it, I could make the entire ordeal go away.

Ms. Rankin paused. Then, whether moved by compassion or mere pity, she handed the evidence back to me. I snatched it from her hand before she could change her mind, and then I promptly tore it into a thousand tiny white pieces. Satisfied the evidence of my sin had been destroyed, I stuffed the pieces deep into the trash next to her desk.

I didn't learn until later that night that guilt isn't so easily erased.

Neither is fear of punishment.

Which is why late that evening, in the dark of my bedroom, I lay in my bed, stomach churning and unable to sleep. I couldn't bear the waiting, the not knowing, the certainty that regardless of the note's shredding, my parents would find out. The teacher would call, a classmate would tell. Punishment was just a matter of time. Once again, the waiting and not knowing proved the worst form of torture.

One or two hours past my bedtime, long after my brother succumbed to sleep and left the day's events behind, I crawled out from beneath my Holly Hobbie bedspread, opened my bedroom door, and padded down the long hallway to the kitchen, where my parents sat at the kitchen table. Then, with the regret of a criminal caught, I confessed my crime to the people who held the power to crush me.

Years later, my parents told me they found the entire ordeal hilarious, their conscience-stricken daughter confessing in the late hours of the night to third-grade note-passing.

But it was anything but funny to me. Still isn't. Behind my agonizing confession sat a terrifying belief that defined my life and my faith for decades:

Love can be lost. And to make a mistake means to lose relationship with those who hold the standard.

My pint-sized self would rather die a thousand deaths than be left all alone.

I find great comfort in the fact that the Bible contains no shortage of complex family dynamics, including Abraham and his family line. He may have been the chosen means of God's covenantal promise, but clearly he didn't escape familial pain and conflict.

When Abraham was the ripe old age of one hundred, Sarah gave birth to their long-awaited son. They named him Isaac, a Hebrew name that means "to laugh." Isaac was flesh-and-blood evidence of God's covenantal love, a promise cut in a sober and terrifying wilderness ceremony. And the first evidence of the fulfillment of that promise was this tiny bundle of human flesh born to a pair old enough to be his great-grandparents. They did indeed laugh.

When Isaac turned forty years old, he married a woman named Rebekah. But Rebekah and Isaac ended up with the same childbearing challenges that Abraham and Sarah had. After years of infertility, Isaac prayed to his God for another laughter-inducing miracle: a baby. God listened, and Rebekah became pregnant, uncomfortably so.

"Why is this happening to me?" she complained.

The words muttered by every mother since the beginning of time. Forever and ever, amen. But I digress.

After her heartfelt prayer, God answered Rebekah with more

blessing than she bargained for: "Two nations are in your womb, and two peoples from within you will be separated; one people will be stronger than the other, and the older will serve the younger" (Gen. 25:23).

Calamitous family conflict even before birth. Have mercy, *twins*. While Rebekah's tummy bulged and stretched, God revealed what His sovereignty had already decided. This time, the evidence of God's Abrahamic covenant would come in a "buy one, get one free" package. And the younger would rule the firstborn.

Did I mention the story is complicated? Enter Esau first, and then Jacob, the second and smaller of Isaac and Rebekah's twin boys. Jacob, bless him, grabbed whatever he wanted, beginning with the heel of his older brother as he exited the birth canal. Holy sibling rivalry. I can only imagine what parent-teacher conferences were like as they grew up.

But it gets worse. To throw a bit of fuel on the embers of a sibling fire, Isaac and Rebekah decided to play favorites: "Isaac . . . loved Esau, but Rebekah loved Jacob" (v. 28).

Ouch.

That kind of parental favoritism messes with a child's sense of security, regardless of whether you're the favored or the rejected.

By Genesis 27 and 28, things aren't good on the family front. Over time, Esau seems to be more insecure than his tough-guy appearance, desperate for his father's blessing and love. And Jacob proves to be a spoiled and manipulative child, willing to deceive those he claims to love to get his way. With the help of his mother, Jacob plots to steal Isaac's blessing on Esau, the firstborn son. After whipping up a convincing costume and doing his best Esau impersonation, he fools his blind father into giving him the firstborn blessing while Esau is making his dad dinner. When Esau discovers what Jacob has done, he erupts in a rage. Jacob may have won the fisrtborn blessing, but he loses his most important relationships in the process.

Fearing her older son will lose his head and her younger son will lose his life, Rebekah packs Jacob up and tells him to run, fast and hard, from the only home he's ever known and to his uncle Laban's house.

Ego and deceit sever family ties. Eden's curse continues.

I'd love to tell you things got better from there, that Jacob learned his lesson. But the drama continued, including Jacob's marrying a pair of sisters—his mother's brother's daughters—loving one more than the other, sleeping with both as well as their two servants, and manipulating his uncle's herds to gather as much loot as he could for himself. Then, caught once again in his deceit, Jacob took his wives and children and fled his angry father-in-law in the middle of the night.

Sound familiar? Dysfunctional family patterns have a way of repeating themselves.

All of this provides the backstory for two pivotal moments that changed Jacob's faith. The first happened when he fled his parents' house. The second when he ran back to it.

The first shows up in Genesis 28. After leaving Beersheba to escape his angry brother, Jacob stops for the night in the middle of nowhere after the sun has set. Then, finding a stone to serve as a pillow, he settles in to sleep. That's when, while camped out under heaven's stars, Jacob has a dream.

In his dream, Jacob sees a stairway reaching from heaven and resting on the earth. On the ladder, the angels of God ascend and descend, representing God's continuous and uninterrupted relationship with His people. While Jacob sleeps fitfully at the base of the ladder, God stands fully awake at the top and speaks: "'I am the Lord, the God of your father Abraham and the God of Isaac. I will give you and your descendants the land on which you are lying. Your descendants will be like the dust of the earth, and you will spread out to the west and to the east, to the north and to the south. All peoples on earth will be blessed through you and your offspring. I am with you and will watch over you wherever you go, and I will bring you back to this land. I will not leave you until I have done what I have promised you'" (Gen. 28:13–15).

Rather than leave him to his mess, God meets him in it. Although Jacob is full of pride and deceit, God reaches for him and firmly establishes the plans of heaven with the disaster of earth. Without first requiring Jacob's reform, God extends a ladder of relationship.

God demonstrates His covenantal love.

When Jacob wakes up and the dream ends, humility finally hits its mark: "'Surely the LORD is in this place, and I was not aware of it.' He was afraid and said, 'How awesome is this place! This is none other than the house of God; this is the gate of heaven'" (vv. 16–17).

Finally, Jacob acknowledges a power greater than his own. In response, he takes the stone he'd used as a pillow and sets it up as an altar, a reminder of what had taken place in that spot. Then, after pouring oil over the stone to establish it as a sacred site, Jacob makes his own promise to follow God.

And he names that place Bethel, "House of God."

I first heard the words *attachment theory* soon after Troy and I added three more children to our family. In hindsight, it would've been helpful to know about it a few decades before.

Two months prior, the second of our three boys graduated from high school, and the third was about to start driving a car. From all appearances, we were approaching the final leg of the parenting years, something we welcomed with no small amount of celebration. Then, on an ordinary weekday afternoon, a phone call shook our world and turned everything upside down. Three preschool children who'd been raised in an environment of addiction, abuse, and trauma needed a place to call home. Twenty-four hours later, we picked them up and made them our own.

One of the best decisions we've ever made.

Even so, it hasn't been easy. I won't go into the story here because I've detailed it elsewhere. Besides, it's not entirely my story to tell. But I will say this. I had no idea what we were in for. Just as a violent earthquake wrecks a building's foundation, early childhood trauma kicks the support structures loose in a child's brain and heart, putting that child in danger of caving in on himself and taking those around him down. It didn't take more than a few days together for me to realize we were in over our heads in rubble.

That's when I started reading everything I could on early childhood trauma and attachment theory.

Simply, attachment theory was developed in the 1950s by a British psychoanalyst named John Bowlby. Bowlby said that babies are born programmed to develop attachment with others as a means to survive. Our longing for strong, attached, healthy relationships isn't optional but absolutely necessary for the surviving and thriving of the human species.

In his research, Bowlby observed—as have any of us who have volunteered in a church nursery on a Sunday morning—that a child who is separated from his mom or dad can become quite unmoored. Screaming, crying, scratching, and clinging are all within the realm of possibility when a child experiences such separation, even if only for the length of a pastor's sermon (albeit some are longer than others). Bowlby set out to understand the why behind a child's strong reaction to separation, and then to determine its implications for child development and growth.

Although Bowlby developed the theory and the term, countless others have studied attachment's importance in the years since, and the dire consequences of its distortion or absence. Books like *Bowling Alone*[12] and *Loneliness: Human Nature and the Need for Connection*[13] dive deep into the cultural and individual implications of humanity's biological disposition to function in safe community. Without getting into all of the science-y, nerdy details (although I happen to be, unashamedly, one of those science-y, nerdy types), I will say that attachment is far more important than most of us realize.

It's a physiological necessity.

Babies are born without any ability to comfort or provide for themselves. They are, in every way, dependent. Far more dependent than that little box on your tax return implies. When an infant has a safe, stable significant other attuned to her needs, she will thrive. Without that attachment, a child may suffer myriad ill effects of mind, brain, and body.

Thankfully, many children are born to parents equipped to care for them. These moms and dads provide food when the baby is hungry, touch when the baby is crying, a dry diaper when the baby is wet, and lullabies and soothing words when the baby has trouble falling asleep. Every need is met, often at record speed. And the baby grows to feel safe within her circle of caregivers. This forms a bond, an attachment.

This explains her temporary turmoil when her mom drops her off in the church nursery for an hour.

Some babies, however, aren't born to loving, safe, attached care-providers. Instead, attention is unpredictable or absent and needs remain unmet. These little ones aren't held when they cry, nor are they comforted when a stomachache, bottom rash, or loud noise upsets them. They are ignored, abused, abandoned. Where God designed connection, these babies are born into a world of detachment or dangerous attachment. They have no one on whom they can depend. So they grow up unmoored, out of sync with the world, and in a chronic state of fear, distrust, and insecurity.

When a creation that is wired up to connect biologically, emotionally, and spiritually learns that connection can't be trusted, there is a wound.

All of us carry this trauma to different degrees. Even the best parents don't get it right. But for children who suffer neglect, abuse, and abandonment, the wound proves far bigger than any one person can heal.

⋄

There are times when I read the Old Testament and struggle to make sense of it. The dysfunctional families, murderous agendas, strange dreams and experiences. It seems left field, far-fetched, impossible. When I look at what God does or doesn't do, I struggle to understand Him. How could a real and loving God act the way He does? I don't get it.

Until a day comes when, somehow, I get a glimpse of the bigger picture, the greater story. Then, if I'm able to stand back if only for a moment, I can see the beauty of the whole.

Generations after Jacob dreamed of a divine ladder connecting heaven to earth, Jesus makes a statement that fits the puzzle pieces together. As He begins a three-year ministry that upsets the religious and rescues the desperate, He gathers a group of twelve messed-up, inconsequential, uneducated men. It is there Jesus gives a head-nod to the dream Jacob experienced so many years before: "Very truly I tell you, you will see 'heaven open, and the angels of God ascending and descending on' the Son of Man" (John 1:51).

Jacob's ladder foreshadowed the greater glory, one that was fulfilled hundreds of years later when a man named Jesus became the established, irrevocable, unalterable connection between heaven and earth.

As fantastical as Jacob's dream was, it remained only the barest hint. Because a day was coming when Jesus' life and death bridged the distance wrought by trauma in the human heart. Jacob's dream wasn't about a ladder or even the angels climbing up and down it. It pointed to God's relentless desire to attach to the people He loves.

He is the bridge connecting the glory of heaven to the humiliation of man. Although fully divine, God chose to put on human flesh—the ultimate expression of humility—in order to be with us.

"As soon as Jesus was baptized, he went up out of the water. At that moment heaven was opened, and he saw the Spirit of God descending like a dove and alighting on him" (Matt. 3:16).

Through Jesus, heaven opened and God landed with two dirty human feet on the same earth where you and I stand.

No matter how hard we may try, we have no ability to reach God. We cannot climb a ladder of our spirituality to touch Him. We can't even get our act together enough to be worthy of Him. Instead, Jesus enters where we dream on stone pillows, running from one crisis and toward another. He meets us there. Not because we deserve it but because His covenant love can't help it.

Later in Genesis, Jacob experiences a second faith-changing event. This time, he is escaping his angry father-in-law and running back home to reconcile, maybe to reconnect with the brother he swindled. Once again, Jacob finds himself alone in the middle of nowhere. And once again, God meets him there: "A man wrestled with him till daybreak. When the man saw that he could not overpower him, he touched the socket of Jacob's hip so that his hip was wrenched as he wrestled with the man . . . Then the man said, 'Your name will no longer be Jacob, but Israel, because you have struggled with God and with humans and have overcome'" (Gen. 32:24–25, 28).

After a long night of struggle, God changes Jacob's name from "he grabs the heel" to "he struggles with God." With that simple name change, Jacob becomes less of an opportunist and more of a warrior, someone God refuses to give up on. Someone with whom God chooses to remain in relationship.

Whereas Jacob named the place of the ladder Bethel, he named the place of his limp Peniel. "The face of God."

As far as I can tell, Jacob walked with a limp the rest of his life. And I can't help but wonder whether Jacob's dislocated hip was as much an altar as the stone pillow he once slept on. God marked him, and his limp became a pin on the map of his story, reminding him of his wrestling match in the black of the night and the God who met him there.

And after all was said and done, Jacob didn't memorialize the wrestling or the wound.

What he remembered was God's face.

When I can't look myself in the face, God turns my head to look at His. His love rescues good families and dysfunctional ones, ego addicts and drug addicts. And though we may wrestle long into the night and wake up with a limp, on the other side of the struggle is a love that will always reach down. And with one glimpse of His glorious face, we'll find new grace and courage to overcome.

As Russell Moore, a Southern Baptist pastor and leader, writes in his book *The Storm-Tossed Family*, "You are not your genealogy. You are not your family tree. You are not your family. After all, if you are in Christ, you are a new creation."[14]

"'Do not be afraid, Jacob my servant, for I am with you,' declares the Lord" (Jer. 46:28).

Lift up your head, Warrior. Every now and then, heaven opens and a hand reaches down to connect the past and the future with a story bigger than our own. Like Jacob's ladder, it hints of a greater salvation, a God who is more relentless than our worst circumstances, and a deliverance that isn't just for one man and his children but for those who have already lived and died and those yet to be born.

Can you see His face? It's the face of a God who sees you where you are.

And meets you there.

ALTAR STONE 3

LOOKING FOR GOD'S PRESENCE IN YOUR LIMP

It's not an easy thing to believe that the face of God could show up in our limp. But when we look for Him, search for Him with all our hearts, we'll find more than we can imagine. What is your limp? What part of your circumstance or story or family tree has marked you, changed you? Whether it is seen or unseen, name your limp. Go ahead, it hurts more to hide it than to tell the truth about it. Then take a deep breath and look for the face of God in it. Having trouble? Ask Him to help you see His dogged presence in the dark of your wrestling match. How has God shown Himself to you not in spite of your struggle but as a result of it? Pray for God to open your eyes to see what you have missed. Then write it down. Mark it. This is your third altar stone.

Uncle Jim and Aunt Ruth lived close . . . They owned a ranch in Pleasant Valley, Arizona. I have such wonderful memories of this time—the ranch was a boy's dream. It had outhouses, a pond filled with frogs, an apple orchard, Indian legends, stories of the cattlemen-sheepmen war, and a shotgun hanging over the fireplace. I remember the wood-burning stove, the old barn, the walnut tree that was so big but not too big to climb. I remember my dad teaching me to fly-fish in Canyon Creek . . .

There were two outhouses (no inside toilets), and I remember having to go outside at night to use the bathroom and there weren't any lights. My imagination would always run wild, and of course, it didn't help that my siblings would choose to use the opportunity to hide around the outhouse and scare me.

—DAD, DECEMBER 8, 2011

CHAPTER 4

A Pillar of Cloud and Fire

A God Who Is with You When You Wander

Earth's crammed with Heaven,
And every common bush afire with God;
But only he who sees, takes off his shoes.

—ELIZABETH BARRETT BROWNING, "AURORA LEIGH"

The trouble is that relying on God has to begin all over again every day as if nothing has yet been done.

—C. S. LEWIS, *LETTERS TO MALCOM, CHIEFLY ON PRAYER*

He stands twenty-two feet tall, perched at the top of a mountain overlooking Denver.

The Sacred Heart of Jesus.

Every time I drive toward the mountains, I see him standing there, glowing white, day and night. With eyes scanning the valley and one hand covering his heart, he lets me know where I am, either sending me off to a weekend adventure or welcoming me back home to everyday life.

It isn't actually Jesus, of course. It's a statue carved in 1954 by an Italian artist, a production of an ordinary man's imagination. Still, when I see him standing there, it pulls me from my sixty-five-miles-an-hour life and reminds me of the one who holds all things in His hands.

The Sacred Heart of Jesus has long been an iconic marker along Colorado's Interstate 70, connecting the city to the foothills and Rocky Mountains on the other side. The statue is part of the Mother Cabrini Shrine of Golden, Colorado, and serves as a peaceful retreat for spiritual seekers to reflect, meditate, and pray. Catholics travel from all over the world to visit Mother Cabrini and Jesus. And although I am not Catholic, I sometimes climb up that mountain to find something I'm looking for.

This is why, during my season of spiritual lostness, I trekked back to the Sacred Heart of Jesus.

The day was warm, the early summer sun filling the cloudless sky. I parked beneath a tree near the convent and gift shop and remained in my car for a minute as I finished off the last of my no-foam latte.

Saint Francis Xavier Cabrini—Mother Cabrini—first fell in love with the property in 1902 when she came to visit her beloved Colorado and local Italian miners and their families. Moved by the needs of so many mining orphans, Mother Cabrini decided to farm the land and create a camp for girls in the summer, a place where they could find healing through fresh air and the care of the farm and animals.

But the property had no reliable source of water aside from one small pond. Every day, the sisters had to haul drinking and cooking water from the stream at the bottom of the canyon below, a chore that became more difficult, especially during the winter months. They were thirsty and needed a solution.

In September 1912, after listening to the sisters complain, Mother Cabrini reportedly said, "Lift that rock over there and start to dig. You will find water fresh enough to drink and clean enough to wash with."

To this day, the spring has never stopped running. And many who have traveled to drink its waters claim to have been healed by its magic.[15]

Latte finished, I climbed out of the car and headed toward the base of the mountain and the stairway that would lead me to the top. I held no illusions about magic water, but I did believe in the healing power of God's presence. I was thirsty for Him. In all the sickness and surgeries and recoveries, I'd grown dry and brittle. I needed God, to be refreshed by His nearness. And I thought perhaps a quiet hour or two spent in meditation might quench my soul.

I climbed one at a time the 373 steps connecting the parking lot to the Sacred Heart of Jesus. Along the way, I stopped at each station detailing Jesus' life, death, and resurrection. Pausing, I took in the artwork, at times sitting on the terra-cotta benches to consider the Jesus who willingly took such a hard journey. I thought about what it meant for Him and what it meant for me.

Although a smattering of other sojourners climbed the stairs with me, there was little noise. Instead, solemn expectation.

I'd crossed the distance for one reason alone.

To find God.

Hanging in my dad's workshop, above his table and tools, meticulously ordered and aligned, was a four-inch by eight-inch wood plaque including three short words painted and finished to a soft shine with polyurethane. The plaque outdated me by a generation. But its motto had been my dad's driving mission for much of his life.

"Work and Pay."

I read those words each time I visited Dad in his workshop. And they reminded me over and again that life is a transaction of work and reward.

In some ways, this has served me well. The greatest gift Dad gave me, second only to his faith, was his work ethic. Those who know me know I'm not afraid of a little sweat. Whether it's writing books and coaching clients, or splitting logs, mowing the grass, and tackling a remodeling project with my husband, a solid day of labor feels good. And I know this is Dad's influence.

But while the motto motivates hard work, it has no place in faith. When "work and pay" bleeds into Christianity and faith, what was meant to give freedom and life turns into a cruel form of slavery.

Recently, while reading *A Hidden Wholeness* by Parker Palmer,[16] I was reminded of an old ranching practice on the Great Plains during a blizzard. At the first sign of a brooding storm, the rancher or farmer tied a rope from the back door of his homestead to the door of the barn. More than a few ranchers had lost their way in a whiteout while tracking to the barn to feed their animals. Frozen to death in the span of one hundred yards.

I know what it's like to feel lost in my own back yard. For four decades, I've wandered the wilderness of my life and faith hanging on to different ropes. Some of those ropes, thanks to the wisdom of my parents and other spiritual mentors, have proved solid. Ropes like a commitment to studying the Bible, the importance of integrity, and the value of serving a church community.

Other ropes, however, have proved to be less lifeline and more bondage. Ropes like legalism, rigidity, and performance-based spirituality. These didn't lead me closer to the warm home of the gospel but farther away from it. I ended up terrified of making God angry or, heaven forbid, doing something that would cause Him to revoke His love. This fear infiltrated every bit of my faith, wrapping tight like a noose around my neck. In a silent but sinister twist of theology, my goodness ceased being a product of a life-giving love relationship with God and instead became a requirement for securing it.

Work and pay. A rope designed to enslave, not set free.

Here's the irony: many of those ropes—the sound ones as well as the sinister—came from the same people. These individuals not only inspired my spiritual growth but also unwittingly contributed to my slavery. Why? Because they're flawed and standing on the outside of Eden's gates too. We were all caught in the same storm of the human experience, trying our best to find our way home.

I'm not comfortable with lostness. I want GPS coordinates, a tried-and-true map of where I stand and where I'm going. Ambiguity feels dangerous to a person accustomed to the safety of black and white. Thus, in my twenties, thirties, and early forties, my faith looked a lot like rule-following. A list of do's and don'ts can feel an awful lot like security. I doubled down and tried even harder to be a good girl, the kind of Christian who compels God's attention. I attended church, signed up for Bible studies, served in multiple ministries, avoided bad language and bad movies.

Then cancer happened, three times. And three more children who had experienced the worst of the human experience moved into our home and needed our help. And the forty years of a rule-following faith could do nothing to bring the healing we all needed. Hard work and strict morality weren't enough.

I needed wholeness, not just holiness. And in spite of my exhausting efforts, I could do nothing to make that miracle happen.

Lost in the swirling blizzard of false theology and relentless Job-like circumstances, I grew desperate and disoriented, and the tether of my faith frayed to the point I feared it might snap. In those dark months after almost dying, when my will to live was lagging, I challenged my long-held beliefs. Was God real? If real, was He good? And could I trust Him?

I didn't know.

The Old Testament—especially the story of the exodus—also tells of ropes and tethers, lostness and bondage. Generations after Jacob and his children died, his descendants—the Israelites—ended up in Egypt subject to a cruel pharaoh who had no affection for God's people.

"The Egyptians came to dread the Israelites and worked them

ruthlessly. They made their lives bitter with harsh labor in brick and mortar and with all kinds of work in the fields; in all their harsh labor the Egyptians worked them ruthlessly" (Ex. 1:12–14).

Bondage of the literal variety. They "groaned in their slavery and cried out, and their cry for help because of their slavery went up to God" (2:23). The wail of an agony pleading for relief. The good news? God heard. And delivered.

"God heard their groaning and he remembered his covenant with Abraham, with Isaac and with Jacob. So God looked on the Israelites and was concerned about them" (2:24–25).

To begin, God spoke from a burning bush to a runaway prince turned shepherd, a man by the name of Moses (Exodus 3). God sent him from his sheep-tending to Egypt, the place he'd fled forty years before, to demand the Israelites' release (Exodus 4). After weeks of negotiations—including the kind of God-orchestrated, catastrophic consequences that gave the Egyptians a taste of the suffering they had caused—Pharaoh relented. He set God's people, the Israelites, free (Exodus 7–12).

Just like that, God rent the ropes that bound His people and tethered them to Himself. No more suffering. No more groaning and wishing for death. Instead, the promise of a new home. And He went with them, becoming the light leading them every step of the way.

"By day the Lord went ahead of them in a pillar of cloud to guide them on their way and by night in a pillar of fire to give them light, so that they could travel by day or night" (13:21).

But Egypt wasn't to be the end of their storm.

First, Pharaoh changed his mind about his new no-slave policy and chased them down in the desert. With the Red Sea spread out in front and an angry Egyptian army at their backs, the Israelites panicked and lost sight of home.

"They were terrified and cried out to the Lord. They said to Moses, 'Was it because there were no graves in Egypt that you brought us to the desert to die? What have you done to us by bringing us out of Egypt? Didn't we say to you in Egypt, "Leave us alone; let us serve the Egyptians"? It would have been better for us to serve the Egyptians than to die in the desert!'" (14:10–12).

In spite of their short-lived celebration, God delivered once again, this time by parting the Red Sea and leading His people straight through the middle of it.

Again, His people exhaled in relief and celebrated their God's faithful presence:

"And when the Israelites saw the mighty hand of the LORD displayed against the Egyptians, the people feared the LORD and put their trust in him and in Moses his servant" (14:31).

"In your unfailing love you will lead the people you have redeemed. In your strength you will guide them to your holy dwelling" (15:13).

But then—you knew it was coming—the desert on the other side of the Red Sea turned out to be quite hot and dry, and the Israelites grew thirsty. And then God's daily manna buffet grew tiresome. They wanted steak, maybe some coleslaw and chocolate cake. Their discomfort blinded them to the bliss of God's nearness, and they turned bitter.

"If only we had died by the LORD's hand in Egypt!" they wailed (16:3).

So God sent quail, a little meat for the barbie.

But again, their belief in God's presence came up short. When God called Moses to meet Him on Mount Sinai for forty long days and nights, the Israelites panicked in his absence, succumbing to doubt once again.

"When the people saw that Moses was so long in coming down from the mountain, they gathered around Aaron and said, 'Come, make us gods who will go before us. As for this fellow Moses who brought us up out of Egypt, we don't know what has happened to him'" (32:1).

In the absence of someone to see and touch, their faith grew weak, their faith rope frayed. By the end of the forty days, Moses returned to see the Israelites dancing and worshiping a gigantic cow made of solid gold.

I could keep going through biblical passages and human generations, but you get the idea. Deliverance by God. Despondency and disobedience by His people. This was their pattern.

As it is for all of us.

Even so. In spite of their long history of screwing up, God never stopped showing up.

"Neither the pillar of cloud by day nor the pillar of fire by night left its place in front of the people" (13:22).

His presence never left. Even when their hearts wandered.

⋄

It's been more than seven years now since Troy and I added three more small children to our family. The preschool children who came to us lost and with such raw wounds are now in their last years of grade school and the first years of middle school. Therapists have now called their early childhood experience "severe abuse and neglect." In the years since they've been ours, we've tried our best to bring some measure of healing to their pain. But the complicated wounds suffered in childhood are the most difficult to heal.

As a result, I now read the exodus story with different eyes. I don't see the Israelites merely as disobedient people; I see wounded people. Wounded as the result of four hundred years of slavery, abuse, hunger, and infanticide. (Yes, really. See Ex. 1:15–16.) That kind of trauma changes a child and an adult.

By the time I'd graduated from high school, Bowlby's attachment theory was gaining wider acceptance and application. While I tried to strap on adult shoes and toyed with thoughts of getting married, further research discovered that early childhood attachments (or lack thereof) significantly impacted subsequent relationships of all types in adulthood. Attachment styles secured in childhood held significant sway over the health of later relationships.

I cannot overstate how helpful this information would've been to me. Alas, I knew nothing of it until my adult relationships showed symptoms of my own attachment wounds.

Over the years, one particular study bubbled to the surface again and again in my search for healing. Beginning in 1995, this study—the CDC-Kaiser Permanent Adverse Childhood Experiences (ACE) Study—went a long way toward establishing the connection between early childhood experiences and adult wellness.[17] To this day, the ACE study remains one of the largest investigations of the long-reaching impact of childhood trauma. To simplify, the ACE study provided a ten-question survey to its participants to identify exposure to different categories of adverse experiences and childhood stress. Each participant was then assigned a score.

The results were stunning.

Two-thirds of participants reported experiencing at least one adverse childhood experience, and 38 percent reported two or more. Even more serious are the associated physiological, psychological, behavioral, and financial repercussions per every additional ACE score. Every individual point increased the participant's risk of alcoholism, depression, poor work performance, and overall health-related quality of life, to name a few. Not to mention an increased incidence of more serious illnesses like autoimmune disease, heart disease, persistent depression, migraines, and cancer.[18]

What happens in childhood doesn't stay in childhood. Just as waves initiated on one side of a pond ripple to the other, the way we attach (or don't) in childhood changes how we see, respond to, and experience life as a whole. This matters even for those who don't experience abuse and neglect. Even the best parents don't offer perfect attachment.

We see ripples of these childhood experiences in something

experts call attachment styles. To simplify, experts have identified three basic styles, and each of us tends toward one of the three. Although you and I learned these styles in childhood, they influence how we relate to, react to, and connect with each other in adulthood.

To begin, children who grew up with consistent, available, and responsive caregivers are more likely to develop what's called a secure attachment style. If that's you, you likely see yourself as capable and worthy of love and, as a result, enjoy a primary relationship as a secure home base from which to explore and experience life. This is the aim, the ideal.

Of course, the ideal isn't real for most of us. Chances are you will see hints of yourself and those you love in the next two attachment styles.

Those who grew up with inconsistent or unpredictable caregivers are more likely to develop an anxious attachment style as adults. Because of the irregular availability of caregivers and the resulting unmet needs, they approach adult relationships with more fear and anxiety. They view themselves as unworthy, unlovable, and often require repeated reassurance and proximity to soothe their fear of abandonment. As a result, they tend to respond to relationship distress with desperate, anxious, clingy, or explosive reactions.

Whereas anxious attachment looks like hypervigilance, the third attachment style looks like hypovigilance. An avoidant attachment style develops when caregivers are detached or unavailable. These children learn to be extremely self-reliant and invulnerable, living behind a wall of self-protection. As adults, they struggle with intimacy and getting close to others, and often are seen as mistrusting, aloof, and distant.

In the Cushatt family, our everyday reality involves trying to help our children unlearn anxious and avoidant responses to relationship and instead learn secure ones. What worked when trying to survive the chaos of their first five years of life no longer serves them well in safety. That means every day we all negotiate both anxious and avoidant attachment reactions, including everything from desperate, panicky, clingy behaviors to flat, detached, aloof ones.

What I didn't expect seven years ago, however, is how parenting through the lens of attachment styles holds a painful magnifying glass on my own flawed reactions in relationship.

Last weekend, I returned from an extended speaking event that kept me away from my family for several days. Although I enjoyed both the opportunity and the people, I missed my family and couldn't wait to head home. Over the phone, they expressed a similar excitement about our reunion.

But for two days after my return, I received a lackluster welcome. My husband didn't serenade me from the driveway, my children didn't throw confetti from the curb. Instead, after a quick hello, they each disappeared to their own agendas. The nerve. I was left lonely and alone. Surrounded by laundry when what I really wanted was love.

Although I'd later recognize my unrealistic expectations, in the moment I felt hurt. And my disappointment felt a lot like rejection.

As a result, I doubled down trying to do things for them: cooking, cleaning, offering to run errands, making cookies, playing a game. Anything to capture their affection and attention.

Then, when my offers were rebuffed and the relationship still felt distant, I shut down, erected an emotional wall, and matched their aloofness with my own.

You see what happened, don't you? Flawed attachment styles temporarily hijacked a family made for connection.

Sounds a lot like the Israelites' hot-cold responses to God in the wilderness.

In the last few years of spiritual lostness, I've discovered my relational Achilles' heel: aloofness. I can deal with displeasure, but I can't handle distance. Distance feels like a death sentence, as if someone has sucked the oxygen from the room and I can no longer breathe. Rather than a cold and indifferent statue that stands at the top of 373 stairs, I need reciprocity, a flesh-and-blood relationship that sees my needs and responds to them. And this is true not only for me. It's true for all of us.

Back in the 1500s, the word *aloof* was a nautical term. With its negating prefix "a-," to turn aloof was to turn the side of the ship away from the shore and into the wind to keep from drifting. Over time, aloof came to mean "distant" or "removed."[19] A person who is aloof turns his back—figuratively or literally—as a means to avoid danger.

While *aloof* may have kept ships safe, it damages relationship. It creates separation when what is needed is connection. As Henri Nouwen writes,

> If there is any posture that disturbs a suffering man or woman, it is aloofness. The tragedy of Christian ministry is that many who are in great need, many who seek an attentive ear, a word of support, a forgiving embrace, a firm hand, a tender smile, or even a stuttering confession of inability to do more, often find their ministers distant people who do not want to burn their fingers . . .
>
> None of us can help anyone without becoming involved, without entering with our whole person into the painful situation, without taking the risk of becoming hurt, wounded, or even destroyed in the process . . .
>
> In short, who can take away suffering without entering it?[20]

We need someone who will enter into relationship with us, someone who loves us more than they fear the risk. As science journalist Donna Jackson Nakazawa reports, "Most psychologists agree that a child has to develop a secure attachment with at least one primary caregiver in order to learn how to effectively regulate her own emotions for the rest of her life, and in order to learn how to become attached in a healthy way in adult relationships."[21] With secure attachments, we're protected. Without them, we're vulnerable, lost in our own back yard.

The secret to healing? The reciprocal presence of at least one safe, stable, significant other.

"Neither the pillar of cloud by day nor the pillar of fire by night left its place in front of the people" (Ex. 13:22).

As lost as you and I feel, God's presence is where it has always been. With us, behind and before.

The last few years felt like a wilderness to me. And much like the Israelites, I responded to my wilderness with desperation one moment and distance the next. Although I longed to trust God and ached for closeness with Him, suffering blinded me like a snowstorm outside my door. Trauma wounded me, altered my ability to attach, made me afraid I'd never find my way back home.

Even so, God never left. Even when I doubted His reality, He stood guard, behind and before. I saw evidence of Him in the authors and scholars who spoke to my broken heart through their words, in the well-worn pages of my Bible that shone with fresh revelation and new light, and in the steadfast friends who made space for my questions without shaming me to silence.

Just as a dilapidated house sometimes requires rebuilding, my faith needed a rebuilding. I needed to learn what to let go of and what to hang on to. The process felt a lot like lostness. But at the other side of the wandering, I finally found the rope that would lead me home.

"There is a light that shines in the darkness, which is only visible there."[22] Barbara Brown Taylor said those words, a woman who, like me, knows a thing or two about wildernesses and wanderings.

She's right, you know. There is a special kind of light that shows up only in the dark. And it looks like a pillar of fire.

A God who never leaves, even when we wander.

ALTAR STONE 4

LOOKING FOR GOD'S PRESENCE IN YOUR WILDERNESS

If you surveyed every Jesus follower, most would reveal their journey with Him to be more of a zigzag than a straight shot. We each endure seasons during which we feel a bit lost. Although we may still believe in God's reality, we may not buy into His personal love. Although our wilderness wanderings may vary in degrees, every one of us is prone to wander. Think of two or three times when you lost your way, stuck in between what was and what would one day be. In hindsight, do you see evidence of God's presence there? How did His pillar of fire shine a light in the dark while you wandered? Pray for God to open your eyes to see what you have missed. Then write it down. Mark it. This is your fourth altar stone.

Over the years, my mother would often . . . find me wherever I was.

One time when I was in the seventh or eighth grade, she came to the [movie] theater and made such a commotion in the lobby that they came into the show and pulled me out to see her. She was drunk, and she stood there with an audience of my friends watching and told everyone I was a hateful son—that I was going to hell since God wouldn't let a son like me into heaven.

—DAD, DECEMBER 8, 2011

CHAPTER 5

A Tabernacle

A GOD WHOSE MERCY CARRIES YOU

I have spent most of my life in recovery from the church.

—PHILIP YANCEY, *SOUL SURVIVOR*

All the beauty we have looked for in art or faces or places—and all the love we have looked for in the arms of other people—is only fully present in God himself. And so, in every action by which we treat him as glorious as he is, whether through prayer, singing, trusting, obeying, or hoping, we are at once giving God his due and fulfilling our own design.

—TIMOTHY KELLER, *WALKING WITH GOD THROUGH PAIN AND SUFFERING*

The purpose of prayer is that we get ahold of God, not of the answer.

—OSWALD CHAMBERS, *MY UTMOST FOR HIS HIGHEST*

I walked downstairs to a living room filled with church leaders. I thought they had gathered to offer encouragement and support.

I was wrong.

Although barely twenty-one, I was still a girl. Attending college, working full time, and living at home, I still wrestled with lingering adolescent confusion and angst. This was exacerbated when, the week before, my entire world imploded in an unexpected crisis.

I'd discovered, at the cost of more innocence, that the man I was engaged to marry was mired in a secret life I knew nothing about. Without going into details that are not mine to share, I was in over my head and devastated by it. What was I to do? I'd dreamed of marrying and having a family of my own. But the deception and unknown scared me. Should I move forward with my engagement or run fast the other way?

It was too much for a young girl to unravel on her own. Moments before, I'd been in my bedroom, face on the floor, overwhelmed and praying. I'd asked God for wisdom, to please walk me through this hard, hard situation. And to show me His love and nearness in a tangible way.

But what awaited me on the other side of that prayer was the opposite of what I'd asked for. I'd hoped the people waiting in my parents' living room—men and women I'd known most of my life—would offer comfort and support. Instead, they'd decided to confront.

They rebuked me. Rather than offer comfort in my crisis, they felt a need to correct a past one. Although I had been a model teenager in many ways—straight A's, no partying or sleeping around, consistent youth group attendance and leadership, mission trips and ministry—I'd grown resentful toward my parents' rigidity. And they'd decided to confront my disrespect.

As a mom, I now look back on that night with inner conflict. I understand the sting of an adolescent's disrespect. But I also understand the normalcy of it, the complex developmental process of impending adulthood and the push-pull learning curve of independence. As parents, our role is to create a safe place where our children can struggle through that transition, to coach them and guide them. Not to crush them.

But in a religious world of black-and-white rules, there is no space for grace, growth, or complex teenage emotions.

The priority? Good behavior. Obedience. Doing what is expected of you every time, without fail. My adolescent confusion and anger could not be tolerated or worked through together. So this group of church leaders neglected connection for the sake of harsh correction.

With tears streaming down my face, I looked at each stern face and asked the question at the core of my pain.

"Do any of you care *why* I feel the way I do? Does it matter to you at all?"

There wasn't even a pause. One man answered for the rest of them. "No, we don't. It doesn't matter. The Bible says you're supposed to respect your parents. And that's what we expect you to do."

And with that, a light inside me went out. My biggest fear was confirmed with his answer to my question.

I didn't matter. Only my obedience mattered.

Several weeks later, I entered a marriage that tore me apart and, six years later, ended in divorce. It's not difficult to see why.

I had nowhere else to go.

As well-meaning as I believe those church leaders were—and yes, I truly believe they did what they thought was right—our time together in my parents' living room that night confirmed two false beliefs I've spent a lifetime trying to reverse.

One, difficult feelings have no place in God's family. To belong I need to shut up and do my job. Stuff my emotions, mitigate my behavior, and maybe, *maybe*, I'll have a place to belong.

And two, love lasts only as long as my obedience. God doesn't have time for wandering, confused, lost people. He loves only obedient people. But the moment I mess up? Love will vanish. Presence will disappear. In its place? Punishment, isolation, and abandonment.

If there is one spiritual practice I have thoroughly failed to master, it is prayer. Not only have I failed to perfect it, I rarely enjoy it. Forty years of following Jesus and I still struggle to pray.

Shocking, I know.

I find prayer dry, difficult, and, at best, producing unpredictable results. And sometimes, when I close my eyes to talk with God, I hear the echo of the judging, critical voices of the past adding volume to my self-criticism. Is it any wonder I struggle to pray?

It wasn't always this way. One of my earliest memories is of an answered prayer. A favorite aunt and uncle were visiting from out of town, and I couldn't contain my excitement at their presence. The grownups sat on the teal-and-green 1970s sofa and I played contentedly on the shag carpet. For a preschool girl hungry for connection, this was as close as she could get to heaven.

Until Dad made an unwanted declaration.

"Michele, it's time for bed."

I was devastated. Knowing I could do nothing to alter my father's directive, I stormed to my bedroom. In the process, I failed to say goodbye to my aunt and uncle. As I lay in my dark bedroom, tears rolling down my cheeks, I felt the full weight of this break in relationship. And I prayed to the God I believed in to give me a second chance.

Please, God, please. Help my aunt or uncle to come into my room. So I can say I'm sorry. And goodbye. Please, God. Please!

Minutes later, when my bedroom door opened and my uncle stood surrounded by light from the hallway, I knew not only that God was real but that I mattered to Him.

This innocent belief remained unchallenged for much of my childhood. I prayed for math tests, boy crushes, and lost car keys. If I had a need, no matter how trite, I asked God to meet it. And often He did.

But then I grew up. And too many desperate, urgent prayers remained unanswered or denied. Prayers for my marriage, my children, my health. And with each apparent disregard for my desperate bedroom prayers, my confident, transactional prayer life turned a bit more sour. Why pray if nothing happens? Why ask God to heal, rescue, and save if I can't count on Him to deliver?

Don't You care?

It is this push-pull of desire and disappointment that has most characterized my prayer life. Friends tell me about vibrant daily prayer lives filled with sweet communion with God and regular evidence of His activity. I want what they seem to have.

Naturally, I concluded I must be doing it wrong. I bought the best books on prayer and became a student of those more educated and experienced than I. But more often than not, the books proved cumbersome, heady, with hundreds of pages of tiny little text detailing prayer's purpose and appropriate practice.

The books often caused more pain and suffering than the practice of prayer itself.

That's when I researched different denominations and methods in the hope of finding the one that would finally work. I listened to sermons on prayer, fasted and observed Lent, laminated prayer strategies and stuck them on my nightstand and in my Bible. I drove to cathedrals, shrines, and prayer centers in the hope of finding the secret to a prayer life that didn't feel so dry. I even scoured my personal life for hidden sin, trying to locate any lecherous thought or motive that might keep a holy God distant.

Sin wasn't hard to find. Why would God want to hang out with the likes of me?

Oh, how I wanted Him, needed Him! But in a strange, sad irony, my tireless pursuit of a formulaic prayer life only pulled me farther away from the object of it. In my attempts to earn God's presence, I stopped enjoying Him.

I missed the forest for the trees.

⋄

It all started with an invitation.

"The LORD said to Moses, 'Come up to the LORD, you and Aaron, Nadab and Abihu, and seventy of the elders of Israel. You are to worship at a distance, but Moses alone is to approach the LORD; the others must not come near. And the people may not come up with him'" (Ex. 24:1–2).

Whoa. A personal invitation to experience God's presence. I'll take three, thankyouverymuch.

In response, Moses rose early the next morning and, after making sacrifices on an altar and reviewing the book of the covenant, climbed Mount Sinai to meet with God.

"When Moses went up on the mountain, the cloud covered it, and the glory of the LORD settled on Mount Sinai. For six days the cloud covered the mountain, and on the seventh day the LORD called to Moses from within the cloud. To the Israelites the glory of the LORD looked like a consuming fire on top of the mountain" (Ex. 24:15–17).

A consuming fire.

Did you catch that? God's presence looked like fire.

I wonder if, in all our twenty-first-century attempts to tame God, we've lost the terror and mystery of Him. The truth is, I've never met anyone who has seen or experienced God as fire. Besides, more often than not, we don't really want a God of fire; we want a God of friendship. A relationship that's easy, convenient, and meets our expectations. But maybe, behind our attempts to make God tangible, we've also made Him too small. And that's not what we really need after all.

When the Israelites looked at the mountain where Moses met with their God, the sight overwhelmed. A fire—a *consuming* fire—covered the mountain. The radiating heat singed their eyebrows, the smoke burned their nostrils. As Timothy Keller recently said, God was the *mysterium tremendum,* the "terrible mystery." The reality of God's presence ignited fear and terror, not teddy-bear-like comfort. The consuming fire confirmed what they already knew to be true.

To be near God was to die.

Just as two flaming swords blocked Adam and Eve from reentering Eden, God's holiness kept His people at a distance.

Everyone except for Moses.

"Moses used to take a tent and pitch it outside the camp some distance away, calling it the 'tent of meeting.' Anyone inquiring of the Lord would go to the tent of meeting outside the camp" (Ex. 33:7).

Then when Moses entered the tent, carrying the messages and inquiries of the people, "the pillar of cloud would come down and stay at the entrance, while the Lord spoke with Moses . . . The Lord would speak to Moses face to face, as one speaks to a friend" (Ex. 33:9, 11).

Face to face. The kind of closeness that makes for intimate relationship. One commentary says these words can be translated "mouth to mouth," meaning God spoke to Moses clearly and directly, without the use of dreams or visions. There was a clarity in God's interactions with Moses, giving him the ability to understand what was expected and how the Israelites were to live in relationship to God.[23]

God invited Moses to enter in, to experience His nearness, as terrifying as it was, in a way the rest of the Israelites couldn't. Although Moses did nothing to deserve it, he longed for God's nearness and asked for it (Ex. 33:13–18). Then when God gave it to him, he responded with gratitude: "Moses bowed to the ground at once and worshiped" (Ex. 34:8).

The consuming fire, although fearsome, was always a worship-inspiring gift.

Via the tent of meeting, Moses played mediator between God and the Israelites. And his extended time seeing God's face changed his own.

"When Moses came down from Mount Sinai . . . he was not aware that his face was radiant because he had spoken with the LORD. When Aaron and all the Israelites saw Moses, his face was radiant, and they were afraid to come near him. . . . When Moses finished speaking to them, he put a veil over his face. But whenever he entered the LORD's presence to speak with him, he removed the veil until he came out. And when he came out and told the Israelites what he had been commanded, they saw that his face was radiant" (Ex. 34:29–30, 33–35).

I envy Moses. I envy his invitation and his access, the apparent ease with which he could schedule a face-to-face with the Almighty. And I envy how that nearness made him radiant. Oh, how I want the same kind of intimacy!

Perhaps this is why my Catholic friends value the practice of confession. At confession, you enter a small, private room—a confessional—where you know a priest is waiting to meet with you. There is a guarantee of presence. Not the presence of God, but at least a representative of God. Prayers and confessions aren't offered in isolation, where it seems they echo off the walls of an empty room. Instead, there's proximity, closeness, and a flesh-and-blood person. And you receive words and advice and absolution in response.

But Moses wasn't the only one who needed a daily dose of God's presence. The entire Israelite camp needed His nearness. So God moved closer still.

"Have them make a sanctuary for me, and I will dwell among them" (Ex. 25:8).

God planned to set up house with His people right where they lived. Not to deliver death but to give life. To a people waiting at the base of Mount Sinai, unable to approach the Consuming Fire, this was good news. And terrifying news.

It must've singed the shock right off their faces.

God initiated the first church-building campaign, the construction of a meeting place to be home to His presence. In the wilderness, that building was a tent, a movable tabernacle. Then once the Israelites reached the promised land, it became a temple.

Exodus (and later Leviticus) details God's instructions to Moses regarding the tabernacle construction, including the layout and design, the tools and materials to be used, how those materials were to be cut and formed, even the specific craftsmen who were to carry out the task and the "articles" that were to fill the inside. Although the tabernacle was to be God's home with His people, His holiness still required some distance. Thus, the tabernacle was to be separated from the rest of the camp by separate inner rooms and thick curtained walls.

This innermost room—the holy of holies—was the center of God's presence. Only three articles occupied this space: a lampstand of seven candles that burned continuously, a table on which sat the "bread of presence," and the ark of the covenant. A container made of pure gold, the ark held the stone tablets of God's covenant law (the Ten Commandments), Aaron's priestly staff, and a jar of manna, God's daily provision of food during the Israelites' forty-year wilderness journey.

Every single one of these items was significant because it represented God's power and provision, and the faithfulness of His presence and deliverance, as well as served as a reminder of the Israelites' promise to obey Him.

But what I find the most compelling about the ark is what sat prominently on top: the mercy seat (Ex. 25:17–22).

Also called the "atonement cover," the mercy seat was thought to be the resting place of God's presence. Made of gold, it included two gold cherubim, one at either end, with their wings spread out like a canopy over the cover. Once a year, in a ceremony performed on the Day of Atonement, the priests sprinkled the blood of sacrifices over the mercy seat to atone for the sins of the people (Leviticus 16). This blood offering served as a reminder of the cost of a broken covenant and Israel's separation from God's presence.

Much the way Eden's bloody animal skins covered Adam and Eve and reminded them of the cost of their sin.

"Then the cloud covered the tent of meeting, and the glory of the LORD filled the tabernacle. Moses could not enter the tent of meeting because the cloud had settled on it, and the glory of the LORD filled the tabernacle. In all the travels of the Israelites, whenever the cloud lifted from above the tabernacle, they would set out; but if the cloud did not lift, they did not set out—until the day it lifted. So the cloud of the LORD was over the tabernacle by day, and fire was in the cloud by night, in the sight of all the Israelites during all their travels" (Ex. 40:34–38).

What was promised to Abraham was tangible in the tabernacle. "The Hebrew word for which 'mercy seat' is the translation is technically best rendered as 'propitiatory,' a term denoting the removal of wrath by the offering of a gift."[24]

For a people recovering from the trauma of four hundred years of slavery and death, the tabernacle became a daily reminder that they'd not been abandoned. Rather than wrath, God gave them mercy.

Himself.

We sat shoulder to shoulder in church, just as we had hundreds of times before. Though he'd left home after high school and we no longer shared Sundays together, a break from a tough semester of college brought him home for the weekend. So we went to church, just like old times.

I can't remember the full sermon that Sunday, and I doubt my son remembers it either. But somewhere in the middle of the message, the pastor scanned the Saturday night crowd and asked a pointed question: "You know you don't have to be good for God to love you, right?"

Was this a rhetorical question? A test? Multiple choice would be easier. Maybe true or false.

No one said a word. It seemed as if we collectively held our breath, waiting for the punchline.

"Let me say it another way." He paused. "With a show of hands, how many of you grew up believing you needed to be *good* for God to love you?"

The congregation came to life as hands raised throughout the auditorium. Men and women, young and old. From the sound of it, I guessed the majority in the room had a hand in the air. Truth is, I didn't look. I was too busy paying attention to what was happening in my own row.

I didn't hesitate when the pastor posed his question. Yes, I grew up believing I had to be good for God to love me, that His love was conditional. This belief drove me well into adulthood, and too often I still slipped back into legalism—toward myself and others.

I held my hand up along with hundreds of others, feeling both sadness at the truth and relief at the camaraderie. I wasn't the only one who'd been duped.

And that's when I noticed my son's arm raised high right next to mine.

My stomach sank, but I was not surprised. Though the only light came from the platform, I tried to see my son's face through the dark.

"I'm sorry, babe," I whispered. "I'm sorry."

Out of all the things I wanted to do right as a mom, this was the big one. And now, when it seemed too late to do anything about it, I discovered I'd blown it.

"It's okay, Mom," he whispered.

I shrugged, smiled. "I know better now," I reassured him, reassured myself.

He didn't miss a beat. "I do too."

Mercy, sweet mercy. I didn't deserve it, I knew. He gave it to me anyway.

Which is what I think God had been trying to tell me about Himself all along.

God's presence doesn't sit in judgment.

He sits in mercy.

He doesn't withhold His compassion until I get all my Christianity right. He doesn't even wait for me to have it all together to show me His kindness. Though my prayers are flawed and my performance unpredictable, though I claim to love Him and can't always understand Him, His mercy carries me. It carries every single one of us, flawed children and parents alike. And the glimmers of His presence cover us like a bottle of glitter upended.

"And we all, who with unveiled faces contemplate the Lord's glory, are being transformed into his image with ever-increasing glory, which comes from the Lord, who is the Spirit" (2 Cor. 3:18).

I now have a chair in my office. A prayer chair. My mercy seat.

Leather, brown, and nestled under glass-globed light. It's a sort of sanctuary, a place set apart. On my shelf sits my Bible and journal, and in the chair's ottoman sit a devotional, a book of prayer liturgy, and the Book of Common Prayer.

Some days I don't make it to the chair. And some days, when I do, I pick up the devotional or one of the prayer books, along with my Bible.

But most days, I simply settle into the leather, wrap myself with a blanket, and close my eyes. Without formula or fanfare, I listen for Him. Part of me will probably always fight the voices of the past, those tired old recordings of criticism and rejection. "Don't You care?" rings in my memory, and I'm still tempted to pull back, afraid of the answer.

But He's teaching me to wait, to resist filling the space with words that haven't served me well. And to allow Him to surprise me with some of His own.

Yes, I care, Michele, He whispers.

My mercy will not fail you, He promises.

I choose to believe Him one more time, to stop trying so hard and instead to bank my entire life on His love. To trust that His mercy will both cover and carry me.

Then I sink deep into His presence. And pray.

> Restore us, God Almighty;
> make your face shine on us,
> that we may be saved.
>
> —PSALM 80:7 (ALSO VV. 3, 19)

ALTAR STONE 5

LOOKING FOR GOD'S PRESENCE IN PLACES OF MERCY

Like gold buried far underground, mercy can be difficult to find when you most need it. We aren't all that skilled at offering it, wounded as we are by those who didn't give it to us. So we become stingy with it, resentful and demanding, refusing to hand out mercy freely, instead portioning it to those we deem deserving. And yet nothing speaks of the presence of God quite as poignantly and profoundly as an unexpected offering of mercy and grace. Consider the moments when you received a gift of mercy. Whether big or small, how might those moments testify to the presence of God with you, right then and right there? Pray for God to open your eyes to see what you have missed. Name it. Then write it down. This is your fifth altar stone.

My dad was an alcoholic who would go months without drinking. But when he would take a drink, it would send him on a drunken binge that could last for days, weeks, or months. Dad didn't go to bars to drink, nor did he drive when he drank. He'd either hide booze around the house . . . or he'd have a friend or taxi driver bring him the booze.

I never knew when I came home from work or school if I'd find him drunk or sober. When he was drunk, he was never mean to [my stepmom] or her children. But he could, on occasion, be mean to me—normally hitting me or kicking me. Seems like he wanted to blame me for something. Most of the time I didn't know why he was mean or why he was drinking. I just thought I had done something to cause it.

—DAD, DECEMBER 8, 2011

CHAPTER 6

A Cleft in a Rock

A GOD WHO IS WITH YOU WHEN YOU REACH THE END OF YOURSELF

Mental pain is less dramatic than physical pain, but it is more common and also more hard to bear. The frequent attempt to conceal mental pain increases the burden: it is easier to say "My tooth is aching" than to say "My heart is broken."

—C. S. LEWIS, *THE PROBLEM OF PAIN*

A waiting person is a patient person. The word *patience* means the willingness to stay where we are and live the situation out to the full in the belief that something hidden there will manifest itself to us.

—HENRI NOUWEN, *ETERNAL SEASONS*

A storm rolled in last night.

The day started bright and warm, the sun filling the robin's-egg sky. Colorado's spring is an artist's palette of color. Nourished by winter's snow, the grass comes in a deep green, lush and thick, before July's heat turns it brown. The perennials push up through the soil to surprise us yet again with daffodil yellows and tulip reds. The crab apple trees' white and pink blooms fill the air with perfume, and cotton candy clouds float like sailboats across the sky.

But then evening rolled around and with it the usual thunderstorm. It's one of the things I love most about Colorado, how a typical day can include as much variation as a year of seasons.

By the time we got home from my son's Little League baseball game, gray, roiling clouds covered the sky. Distant thunder could be heard, although its full punch had yet to be unleashed. I didn't pay much attention to it, accustomed as I am to Colorado's changing weather. Instead, we went inside, helped the kids get ready for bed, tucked blankets around them, kissed foreheads, said prayers. Then I retreated to my own bed, crawled under the covers, and pulled out a book.

Soon I could hear the wind pick up and whip our backyard trees against the windows. Then lightning flashed, followed by thunder's angry response. For me, it formed the perfect backdrop to a little late-night book reading.

Not so for my ten-year-old son.

When I heard the first loud burst of thunder, I thought about him, wondered if he was okay. Hearing nothing, I continued reading.

But then, minutes later, a flash of lightning followed by an explosion of thunder shook my windows.

That's when I heard my boy screaming.

This wasn't the typical cry of fear and uncertainty. His was the screaming of one who believes he's going to die. I flew out of bed and ran toward my bedroom door. When I opened it, I saw him.

Balled up on the carpet in a corner of the upstairs loft, rocking back and forth. He continued to scream, tears streaming down his face, his eyes those of an animal. He didn't see me, even though I stood right in front of him. He was hostage to his terror, consumed by the monster this thunderstorm had become.

Although I stood only a few feet away, he felt utterly alone, unable to see what was so plain. So I pulled him up, wrapped my arms around his body, laid my cheek on the top of his head, and whispered into his ear. "It's okay, buddy. It's okay."

My touch and my presence finally broke through his isolating fear. He continued to rock, but now I led the dance. Back and forth, back and forth. My hands rubbed his back and arms without loosening their grip. He melted into my nearness. I whispered in his ear. "I'm not going to let anything happen to you, I promise."

His screams stopped, even as his tears continued. He whimpered, shuddered, and we kept holding each other.

"Remember what I told you last time?" He didn't speak. "Look at my face." I pulled back so he could see me. "I'm not afraid, not at all. Everything is okay. It's just a thunderstorm."

He stilled, settled. I continued to hold him.

After a few more minutes, I asked him if he was okay. He nodded. I led him back to his bedroom and helped him into bed, pulling the covers back over the top of him and tucking them around his sides, doing my best to nestle him into the comfort of cotton and weighted blanket.

"The thunder will probably continue for a short time, okay?" I could see him nod in the shadows. He was trying so hard to be strong. "But remember my face. I'm upstairs with you, and I'm not going anywhere. I promise." I pushed his hair back, checking one last time to make sure he was okay.

And he was. Like a storm that blusters in but then evaporates, my son's terror had vanished. It was as if he was a different child altogether. Spent and exhausted, but at a place of tenuous peace. For now.

I shut his door and headed back to my room. And then it hit me: Watching him was like seeing the boy my dad had been. And watching him was like seeing myself, the girl caught in storms of her own. His terror looked a lot like mine.

I've spent more than my share of dark nights curled up and alone, screaming at a storm raging outside the window of my life, knowing I could do nothing to bring it to a stop.

But still I waited for someone to find me rocking and weeping, to lift me up, to hold me close and tell me everything was going to be okay.

•⊱◇⊰•

There was a time I doubted the validity of post-traumatic stress disorder (PTSD). Until I went to the dentist a few months after cancer.

One moment I was sitting down in a chair for a replacement filling and cap, and the next moment I was hyperventilating in a near panic. The dentist and hygienist looked bewildered, confused by my reaction to a routine procedure. Not only would it be over in a handful of minutes, I'd done it before. My reaction didn't reflect my circumstances. And although I knew this intellectually, I couldn't do anything about my physical response to it. I was at the mercy of memory.

Somehow, I managed to get through the appointment, as well as several other dental visits since. But after surviving head and neck cancer, I no longer respond to medical appointments with nonchalance. I now must dig deep for emotional resilience and allow space for recovery. Each time, I return home exhausted, hands shaking and tears brimming. Even when I know everything is okay.

Signs of my trauma show up in other ways. Each year, during the months of November through March, I struggle to sleep. Those are the months when cancer showed up—in 2010, in 2013, and again in 2014. I often have nightmares during the holidays, either reliving my almost dying or enduring a new diagnosis that requires the same suffering. Each time, I wake up in a sweat. And it takes me a full day to convince myself it was only a dream.

And then there are the random encounters, online or in person, with people who bear the same scars that I do. And while my heart wants to connect with them, my body rebels against it, as if their proximity stirs up too many memories. I find myself either on the verge of anger or tears, or fighting an urge to run away as fast as possible.

A few weeks ago, while I was getting blood drawn for yet another blood test, the phlebotomist told me a story of her son. In early childhood, he endured a freak accident that nearly killed him. She spent months next to his bedside, helping him through multiple surgeries and hospitalizations and nursing him back to health. He's now in his late twenties, married and with children, and his medical trauma sits two long decades in the past. Even so, he told her about a recent routine physical and blood workup. When the nurse ripped open a packet containing an alcohol swab to clean his skin, the smell sent him into a panic. He experienced a rapid heart rate, difficulty breathing, and an overwhelming sense of terror. All because of the familiar smell of alcohol. Twenty years later and his body remembers.

It took my own experience with PTSD—first with my youngest children and then with myself—to recognize that traumatic responses aren't reserved only for Vietnam veterans and victims of violent abuse. Neglect, accidents, a family death, and significant medical crises can all mark a body. Then gender, biology, personality, and various other hidden factors can individualize the traumatic experience. This means several individuals who experience the same circumstance may respond in different ways. Regardless, one response doesn't make any other less valid.

Ignoring or minimizing trauma and responses to it does nothing to help a person heal. I know this now. Within three months of almost dying, I resumed all of my responsibilities at home and dove back into traveling, writing, and working. My compulsion baffles me, why I thought I needed to bootstrap my way through each day, stuffing my feelings so deep within I could pretend, temporarily, that they didn't wound me as they did. And although this determination to move forward saved me in one regard, the trauma of what had happened would not be ignored. Like cancer, it only grew with my lack of sober attention.

One of the most dangerous Christian practices (and expectations) is the compulsion to present a put-together, unflappable faith. On the whole, we haven't done a very good job of making space for a struggle that lasts longer than we think it should. We may give the struggler grace for a day, a week, a month, a year. But sooner than later, we decide it's high time she pulled it together. This pressure—whether spoken or unspoken—only pushes the sufferer to hide and neglect the long, hard process of healing.

The night in the basement, holding the pain reliever while wondering if suicide would be my only real relief, was the result, in part, of this pressure to perform. For months I had tried to stay strong, keep myself together, present a tough, faith-filled front. But eventually, I ran out of fight. I could no longer muscle my way through my reality.

In the years since, I've experienced too many other dark nights when the thought of death seemed to be my only out. But how could I tell those close to me about the black hole that swallowed me? How could I let them know how desperately I wanted it all to end? Good Christian girls aren't supposed to toy with such thoughts. To reveal the truth would invite more disappointment and shame. And I'd already had enough of both. The pressure I felt came from within and without, but the result was the same. I felt alone in my nightmare, too embarrassed and ashamed to admit I needed help.

Although it was painful, I feel a measure of gratitude for my descent into the dark, because it helped me to see what I needed to see. There was no pretending anymore. No muscling through the losses. Instead, I needed to honor the pain by telling the truth about it, to myself and to others. I needed to see my circumstances for what they were and validate my experience of them.

And I needed to admit, after years of pushing hard through too many impossible circumstances, that I'd finally reached the end of myself.

⊱⊰

There's an oft-used cliche that goes something like this: "God will never give you more than you can handle." I have a few things to say about this claim, but I'll begin with this: It's a load of garbage. It may roll off the tongue reeeeaaal niiiiiice, but it is a big, fat lie.

In spite of the number of times I've been the unwilling recipient of that mantra, I've experienced more than I can handle more than once. Each time, in spite of my extraordinary efforts, I had nothing left to give. No tools, no insights, no solutions, no strength. My characteristic sleeve-rolling, hard-work-and-determination grit dissolved. Struggle and suffering had taken me under. I was flat-faced on the ground. Period.

But don't take my word for it. The Bible is filled with stories of those bent in two under the weight of hard circumstances.

Take Elijah for example.

Elijah was a prophet, a devout one. In an age of paganism, rebellion, and persecution, Elijah served God with passion and fearlessness. Determined and obedient, he delivered God's words to a stubborn horde of Israelites again and again, urging them to turn back to God. He even dared to confront King Ahab and his wicked wife, Jezebel, something that required not a little amount of courage considering their penchant for murdering God's prophets. They turned their sights on Elijah, the "troubler of Israel" (1 Kings 18:17).

Rather than cower, Elijah challenges Ahab and his false prophets to a duel—a showdown between their god, Baal, and Elijah's God. When the day arrives, 450 prophets of Baal stand against a lone Elijah, the last of God's prophets. The 450 prophets of Baal pray like champs. No god replies from the skies. But when Elijah prays a single, sincere prayer, God comes down in a consuming fire (1 Kings 18).

I'd call that a decisive victory. *Score.*

At this point, Elijah expects Ahab, Jezebel, and the Israelites to come to their senses, to turn from their wickedness and once again follow God. But that's not what happens.

"Now Ahab told Jezebel everything Elijah had done and how he had killed all the prophets with the sword. So Jezebel sent a messenger to Elijah to say, 'May the gods deal with me, be it ever so severely, if by this time tomorrow I do not make your life like that of one of them'" (1 Kings 19:1–2).

Terrified, Elijah runs for his life (v. 3) all the way from Jezreel to Beersheba, a distance of about a hundred miles. Then leaving his servant behind, he continues another full day's journey into the wilderness alone. Because some disappointments don't allow space for company.

There, collapsed under a broom bush, Elijah reaches the end of himself.

"'I have had enough, LORD,' he said. 'Take my life; I am no better than my ancestors.' Then he lay down under the bush and fell asleep" (vv. 4–5).

Elijah's bush wasn't all that different from my basement. Despair. Frustration. Disappointment. Exhaustion.

Enough, Lord.

I've lost track of how many times I've said similar words.

The doctors' appointments. The therapy appointments. The conflicts and chronic pain, the headaches and heartaches. The praying, praying, praying and trying, trying, trying only to experience more obstacles, more pain, more confusion.

Enough, Lord. Please. Take my life.

Life often feels like a series of one-hundred-mile days. While I've never had a price on my head, I know what it feels like to pay a high price to live. Like Elijah, there are days when my enthusiasm over my mighty God is tempered by the reality that He doesn't always behave the way I expect Him to.

He doesn't always take the pain away.

He doesn't always cure the illness.

He doesn't always restore the relationship, resolve the conflict, deliver peace and rest.

Buried in frustration and defeat, I collapse into despair, questioning myself even more than I question Him. Surely I've done something wrong. I'm not the faith giant I'd hoped I'd be. Instead, I'm no better than any other struggler, weary and flat-faced.

At this point someone invariably offers me the load-of-garbage maxim. *God will never give you more than you can handle.* The irony? They throw it as a life preserver, hoping to save me from drowning in my circumstances. Instead, the cliche lands like a two-ton weight, finishing me off.

Which is why it matters to me how God responds to Elijah's despair. Rather than a worthless cliche, He offers Elijah comfort.

"All at once an angel touched him and said, 'Get up and eat.' He looked around, and there by his head was some bread baked over hot coals, and a jar of water. He ate and drank and then lay down again. The angel of the LORD came back a second time and touched him and said, 'Get up and eat, for the journey is too much for you.' So he got up and ate and drank" (1 Kings 19:5–8).

What does God do?

He doesn't rebuke him.

He doesn't quote Scripture at him.

He doesn't tell him to get his act together or his butt in church.

He doesn't tell him how much worse it could be.

And He doesn't tell him that He will never give him more than he can handle.

There is no bootstrapping, guilt-tripping, manhandling, heavy-load-throwing.

Instead, God touches him. And feeds him. Twice.

Skin to skin, a tangible acknowledgment of presence.

And bread hot out of the oven. Comfort food. Maybe a casserole with extra cheese. Likely a pan of double-chocolate brownies.

Nourishment of body and soul.

Why?

Because the journey is too much for you.

•⊱◇⊰•

Strengthened body and soul, Elijah brushes himself off and heads out on another trip. His problems aren't resolved and his heart still hurts. He's confused, frustrated, and doesn't understand the God he loves. But a little food and rest go a long way.

So Elijah heads to the one place he hopes will offer answers. First Kings 19 says the journey takes him forty days and forty nights as he hoofs a distance of just under 250 miles. Desperate, Elijah finally ends up where he wants to be, where he *needs* to be.

Mount Horeb. The Mountain of God.

Elijah finds a cave, settles in, and spends the night. Once again, rest. He needs it for what he's already endured and for what is yet to come.

First Kings doesn't provide any direct explanation why Elijah traveled such a distance to visit a mountain. I have a pretty good idea, but I'll get to that in a moment. First let's talk about what happened when Elijah got there, sometime after that first night of cave-dwelling.

"The word of the Lord came to him" (v. 9). God speaks. And Elijah is finally ready to listen.

"What are you doing here, Elijah?"

I find this question laughable, as if God didn't already know Elijah's purpose better than he did. In a recent sermon, Timothy Keller said it this way: "God never asks questions to get information. He asks questions to give *you* information."[25]

Indeed. Hidden in God's question sits the information Elijah is looking for. Elijah answers with all the honesty and heart you'd expect from a man down on his luck and despairing of life.

"I have been very zealous for the Lord God Almighty. The Israelites have rejected your covenant, torn down your altars, and put your prophets to death with the sword. I am the only one left, and now they are trying to kill me too" (v. 10).

I've done so much for You, God. Remember? Remember how tirelessly I've served You and sacrificed for You? Aren't You going to do something?

I'd love to pull on my high-and-mighty pants at this point and comment on Elijah's obvious self-righteousness and sense of entitlement. Unfortunately, he sounds too much like me. Driven by my performance and addiction to results, I expect all of my spiritual math to add up. If I do all of this, I expect God to do all of that. When that doesn't happen, I become disappointed in and indignant at a God who is passive while circumstances turn sour. Like a child raging against a storm he cannot control.

Once again, I expect God to berate Elijah, maybe offer him a solid slap upside his head. Instead of rebuke, however, God first gives him presence.

"'Go out and stand on the mountain in the presence of the Lord, for the Lord is about to pass by.' Then a great and powerful wind tore the mountains apart and shattered the rocks before the Lord, but the Lord was not in the wind. After the wind there was an earthquake, but the Lord was not in the earthquake. After the earthquake came a fire, but the Lord was not in the fire. And after the fire came a gentle whisper. When Elijah heard it, he pulled his cloak over his face and went out and stood at the mouth of the cave" (vv. 11–13).

I believe this is why Elijah traveled 250 miles to camp out in a cave. In the absence of answers, he craved God. So he headed to the place where, generations before, God had delivered Himself to another man searching for His presence.

Moses. Only, at that time, Mount Horeb was called by a different name—Mount Sinai.

"'You have been telling me, "Lead these people," but you have not let me know whom you will send with me . . . If you are pleased with me, teach me your ways so I may know you and continue to find favor with you. Remember that this nation is your people.'

"The LORD replied, 'My Presence will go with you, and I will give you rest.'

"Then Moses said to him, 'If your Presence does not go with us, do not send us up from here . . . Now show me your glory'" (Ex. 33:12–15, 18).

God agrees to do exactly as Moses asks. He sends His presence. And He shows His glory.

"When my glory passes by, I will put you in a cleft in the rock and cover you with my hand until I have passed by" (v. 22).

A cleft in the rock. A cave that many Bible scholars believe may have been the same cave Elijah retreated to when life grew bigger than he could handle.

I didn't expect the loneliness of suffering.

In all the preparations and appointments and conversations, that part never came up. And yet that part proved as powerful and unmanageable as the pain.

It's not that friends and family members didn't try to share in it. They did and do—bless them—asking questions and spending long hours listening and attempting to understand.

But I've learned that no matter the hours and days and weeks I invest in trying to explain the complexities and consuming loss, I can find no words equal to the task. Try as they might to understand, a witness to a hard journey can't know what it's like to walk it. It's like looking at photographs of a marathon and believing you know what it feels like to run it.

Instead, from a place of relative distance, the well-intentioned simply see the miracle of life that is you. They see how suffering could've swallowed you whole. And how, somehow, it didn't. For that reason, they don't see reason to mourn; they see cause for celebration.

Still, for the person who suffers, for the one who endures the unthinkable, grief requires a reckoning. The only way to arrive at honest celebration is to simultaneously allow yourself honest lamentation. Those who suffer will tell you without hesitation: to live after loss comes at steep cost.

Someone recently asked me, "What's the hardest thing for you right now?"

It didn't take me long to answer.

"The choice I make every day to wake up and live."

Yes, there is a deep loneliness in suffering. Whether it's a terminal disease, a chronic illness, the loss of a child, or the irreparable severing of a relationship, suffering brings with it an otherness. Perhaps that is both the burden and the gift. For in this lonely place we learn how to keep company with others who find themselves there.

It's easy to assume that life comes back once the crisis is past. But life never comes back. New life can grow, and I see evidence of that fact. But new life can grow only as it is watered by grief's tears.

I'm going to tell you something, and you won't like it any more than I do. But we both need to hear it.

God's presence is where the pain is.

He's in the losses and diseases and questions. He's in the plans that fail and relationships that refuse to heal. He is with you when you hurt and cry and pout and walk away. And if you and I want to be with Him, we need to stop raging long enough to hear Him whisper into the wound we so desperately want Him to heal.

Recently I read an article by pastor John Piper that spoke healing and hope to my empty heart.

"God is glorified in worship not only by those who come full, but also by those who come desperately needy and pinning all their hopes on meeting God. The same heart of worship that says, 'Thank you,' and, 'Praise you,' when full also says, 'I need you, I long for you, I thirst for you,' when empty. It is the same savoring, the same treasuring."[26]

There are days when God seems hard to find. I weary of the search and want to collapse beneath a bush and dream of heaven. On these hard, hard days, I can't always feel Him. Pain, on the other hand, is impossible to miss. It's as close as my neighborhood or the nine o'clock news. As close as my own throat every time I swallow.

In those moments, I want a God who shows up in earthquakes, wind, and fire. I want a God of fireworks in the sky and visions of Jesus on my toast. I want the sensational and spectacular, something bigger and more powerful than all the pain.

And yet I suspect God knows better than to give me such experiences. We have a way of worshiping things that never last. And the one who holds this crazy world in His hands knows we need far more than a fifteen-minute light show to get through the hard reality of everyday life.

We need a person. A person who holds us while we're rocking back and forth in the loft. A person who touches our heads and feeds us bread. A person who holds us even when we can't see Him.

"Come to me, all you who are weary and burdened, and I will give you rest," Jesus says (Matt. 11:28).

He doesn't tell me that I should feel different, that I should be doing more, that I have no reason to feel the way I do. He would be within His rights to say all of this, without apology. I'm as self-righteous and entitled as anyone. Instead, He touches me, feeds me.

Come, eat. For the journey is too much for you.

Life *is* more than we can handle. And although some days you and I can do little more than collapse onto the floor, there is one who whispers in our ears. He's not always showy, but He's always rock solid. I sink into Him, stop the running and rocking. I decide to hide myself in this cleft in the rock, right here, in the middle of the storm.

Look at My face, He says. *I'm not afraid. You're going to be okay.*

And the last thing I think as my soul slides off into peace is that, perhaps, this is why He allowed me a life that is far more than I can handle.

That way I'd know—and finally believe—He can handle every bit of it.

ALTAR STONE 6

LOOKING FOR GOD'S PRESENCE WHEN YOU'VE REACHED THE END OF YOURSELF

It is often when we most need reassurance that we can't find a scrap of it. Perhaps it's our pain that blinds us to compassion's presence. But our compromised vision does not mean a lack of God's affection. With prayer and a keen eye, spend some time thinking about your darkest and most difficult seasons. Maybe it is the season you're in right now, which makes it the perfect time to do a little mining. What glimpses do you see of God's nearness to you, even if you can't feel Him? If you're struggling to see any glimmers of Him, ask a trusted friend to lend you her eyesight. Ask her if she sees any hints of God's presence with you during this particular season of spiritual hunger. Pray for God to open your eyes to see what you have missed. Then write it down. Mark it. This is your sixth altar stone.

When my mom left my dad, she moved away with me and my sister to the Phoenix area. My dad told me that she was spending her time in bars drinking and . . . "introducing" my sister to men. He wasn't too happy about this but didn't seem to try to do anything about it . . .

I lived somewhere in the slums of downtown Phoenix. The apartment we lived in was joined together with three or four others, the floor of the apartment was mostly dirt and the front door didn't lock. Mom left my sister and I alone, sometimes for days. The neighbors would sometimes share food with us until Mom would return home. We had this mongrel dog . . . One day he brought a bone home that had some fat and meat on it. My sister and I [were] hungry so we took the bone from him and put it in a pot with water, cooked it, and ate what we could.

—DAD, DECEMBER 8, 2011

CHAPTER 7

An Incarnation

A God Who Is with You in Your Humanity

You are called to unity. That is the good news of the Incarnation. The Word becomes flesh, and thus a new place is made where all of you and all of God can dwell. When you have found that unity, you will be truly free.

—HENRI NOUWEN, *THE INNER VOICE OF LOVE*

One of the things you find in people who haven't suffered much is that they tend to believe in propriety.

—DALLAS WILLARD

Being able to feel safe with other people is probably the single most important aspect of mental health; safe connections are fundamental to meaningful and satisfying lives.

—BESSEL VAN DER KOLK, *THE BODY KEEPS THE SCORE*

It was only a month or two after cancer treatment ended when I stumbled into her office, midmorning on a weekday.

I had a 10:00 a.m. appointment, and I arrived with a few minutes to spare. We'd covered a lot of ground together over the six or seven years of our relationship. She the counselor, me the student. Although I typically made it to her office only a handful of times each year, I knew the current crisis likely required more processing and healing. And I trusted her.

So I made an appointment as soon as I was well enough to drive myself to her office and sit for fifty solid minutes.

Settling onto her couch felt like coming home. And although the critical voice in the back of my head tried to shame me for landing in a counselor's office once again, I did my best to ignore it and embrace the comfort of being in a safe place.

We spent the first few moments catching up. Of course, she could see the changes. The tracheostomy opening in my neck, covered by a thick white bandage so I could speak. The red-raw skin and scabs on my chest and neck from the radiation burns. The hair cut short to hide how much had fallen out. The clothes that hung off a body that was a fraction of its size.

And there was my speech. The moment I opened my mouth, she could hear the difference. The scratchy tone. The lisp and slurring. I no longer sounded like the professional communicator who'd sat in her office in the years before, the woman featured on podcasts, radio programs, television. Instead, a stranger.

Bless her, she didn't say a word. She settled into her chair and gave us both a minute to catch our breath.

"So. Michele. How are you doing, really?"

I'm always hesitant to spill my guts in a counselor's office. I realize this makes no sense. Gut spilling is what they're paid for. But the process is ugly. Besides, I'd much rather be asking the questions.

There I was, marred and scarred, shuffling half-dead through my broken life. And I wanted to shoot the breeze rather than expose the hard stuff just under the surface.

"Oh, I'm fine. You know, making progress. One day at a time."

More like one minute—one second—at a time. Hours were too big to tackle.

She asked me a probing question, something to nudge open the door to deeper conversation. I likely squirmed on her couch, wrestling with how much I wanted to say, how much would be enough. Besides, I feared that once I breached the dam holding back the memories, I'd never recover.

Before I could come up with a careful answer, a wave of nausea hit, hard and fast like a tsunami. It came so swiftly I had no time to plan. One moment I was plotting my mature, responsible answers to her questions. The next moment I was looking for a toilet. After five years of cancer and a half year of treatment, I knew I had less than sixty seconds to escape disaster.

The bathroom sat on the other side of a waiting room filled with people, three doorways and a long hallway away. Too far.

"Do you have a garbage can or something? I'm not feeling so great."

It took her only a second to recognize the situation and jump into action. She grabbed her wastebasket and handed it to me.

A *wicker* wastebasket.

What followed over the next moments left me sick with embarrassment for months. Unable to control the nausea that had plagued me night and day, I vomited. Everywhere. First into her leaky wicker basket as I held it over her ornate office rug, and then making a trail through her office on the way to the small kitchen sink where she brewed her morning coffee.

Vomiting isn't enjoyable for anyone. But for a woman who'd lost her tongue, whose mouth and neck were still covered with burns, and whose throat was marked with a tracheostomy opening that refused to heal, it was not only painful but dangerous. Choking was a real possibility.

To her credit, she stayed close, trying to help in any way she could, her eyes brimming with compassion.

But I felt humiliated. Who desecrates their counselor's office in the first fifteen minutes? Therapists expect a little gut spilling, but this was a bit too much.

"I'm fine, I'm fine," I mumbled, wiping my mouth, followed by multiple I'm-sorrys.

It's remarkable how easily I slipped into nonchalance, doing my best to pretend everything was okay. As if the burned, emaciated body hovering on the edge of death wasn't a big deal. I'm a fighter, always have been—always had to be. Determination is my badge of honor, proof to the world that I'm not wasting my skin.

Stuffing my mortification, I did my best to clean up my mess and leave no evidence of what had just taken place. After twenty minutes or so, we'd settled back into her office. And I continued our conversation as if nothing had happened.

Only something had happened. A lot of somethings.

To tell the truth would make a mess, I knew. But would anyone stick around long enough to help me clean it up?

The answer to that question was the one I was most afraid of.

⁂

That wasn't the last time I barfed in my therapist's office. Although I'm happy to report that the barfing I've done since hasn't required a basket, wicker or otherwise.

Most of my purging recently has been of the emotional and spiritual variety. A mining of my story, including childhood, complicated relationships, and cancer. But don't be fooled—it hasn't been any less messy. As it turns out, almost dying has a way of dredging up everything you've tried to ignore in the decades before.

As a result, I could no longer tolerate the trite and cliche, wicker platitudes and shallow memes. I dismissed with not a little disdain anything that promised "Three Steps to This!" or "Four Strategies to That!" Pain taught me that life and faith are far more complex than we give them credit for. And to stuff and oversimplify not only exacerbates the suffering of those in the middle of crisis but keeps us in a place of spiritual isolation and immaturity, in spite of how quickly we quote verses and spout slogans.

Trauma expert Bessel van der Kolk says mere proximity to others isn't enough to create a sense of safety or to calm our body's response to pain and trauma. We need something more.

"The critical issue is *reciprocity:* being truly heard and seen by the people around us, feeling that we are held in someone else's mind and heart. For our physiology to calm down, heal, and grow, we need a visceral feeling of safety. No doctor can write a prescription for friendship and love."[27]

That's why I felt myself drawn to Christian voices—near and far—who weren't afraid to do a bit of barfing themselves. Close friends who didn't mind authenticity. And writers like Brennan Manning, Barbara Brown Taylor, C. S. Lewis, Philip Yancey, and Henri Nouwen.

It was during this season that I dove into my first Nouwen writings, beginning with *The Return of the Prodigal Son* and followed closely by *The Inner Voice of Love*. Written at a time of deep emotional and spiritual crisis, both books read as if Nouwen had pulled up a chair next to mine. He loved God and loved God's people deeply, as I did and do. But he also fought difficult spiritual battles, including loneliness, depression, doubt, despair. The two halves existed simultaneously, and I started to see how the honesty of the latter deepened the authenticity and sincerity of the former. Rather than deny his humanity, he owned it, wrestled with it, invited me into it. In the process, his God became bigger, more powerful, and more present. Both for himself and his reader—me.

"Where you are most human, most yourself, weakest, there Jesus lives," Nouwen wrote.[28] For so long I'd believed that my fallibility and weakness were turnoffs to God, that if I wanted to experience more of God, I needed to pull myself together and become more suitable for His nearness.

Nouwen's honesty challenged this belief and urged me to consider that God might, in fact, feel great tenderness toward me. He reminded me that my humanity comes as no surprise to God. And that the only way to truly approach Him is not in a confident parade of holiness but in the stumbling kneeling of humility. I could lay bare all the weakness, confusion, doubt, despair, and rebellion I'd tried so hard to hide.

To Him, I am not a mess to clean up but a child to love.

I soon discovered, however, that not all Christians share my affinity for honest, humble voices. One day, while reading Nouwen, I shared a quote on social media. A reader offered a rebuke: "I love and appreciate the writing, but I would *not* quote Henri Nouwen."

She believed Nouwen's humanity disqualified him. His struggles and failures meant he had nothing to offer and she had nothing to learn. I shook my head in disappointment and wanted to warn her against reading anything of mine. Although Christians claim to be saved by grace, we don't always offer it.

Nouwen isn't the only one we shun because he missed the holiness mark. Like restaurant inspectors whose job is to find anything unworthy of consumption, we refuse to listen to, learn from, or connect with anyone who proves to be below the acceptable level of flaw.

God's grace is an ocean, we proclaim—except for those who again and again fall into pits of depression, alcoholism, divorce, suicide, promiscuity, addiction, or any number of other vices. Failure can be forgiven, we preach—as long as it happens only once and isn't too big. But those who repeatedly wrestle against human weakness have no place in Christian conversation. They are marked as unreliable voices on this complex journey of faith. Men and women who fight a hard war against sin (and sometimes lose) can't be trusted to teach us anything about Jesus.

"To some who were confident of their own righteousness and looked down on everyone else, Jesus told this parable: 'Two men went up to the temple to pray, one a Pharisee and the other a tax collector. The Pharisee stood by himself and prayed: "God, I thank you that I am not like other people—robbers, evildoers, adulterers—or even like this tax collector. I fast twice a week and give a tenth of all I get."

"'But the tax collector stood at a distance. He would not even look up to heaven, but beat his breast and said, "God, have mercy on me, a sinner"'" (Luke 18:9–13).

Having spent time in the dark, dank sewer of human frailty, I've found I want to hear from those who've spent time there themselves.

How can those who need no mercy offer it?

And how can those who have never known the stench of suffering and doubt tolerate the one who reeks of it?

In his bestselling book, *The Body Keeps the Score: Brain, Mind, and Body in the Healing of Trauma,* Bessel van der Kolk delivers a powerful yet simple insight for those who've suffered relational trauma: "Secure attachment develops when caregiving includes emotional attunement."[29]

Somewhat unsure of the word "attunement," I looked it up for a more precise meaning. According to Merriam-Webster, *attune* is a verb that means "to bring into harmony; to make aware or responsive."[30]

And that's when my brain exploded with the implications. Emotional attunement involves bringing two individuals into harmonious, connected relationship by being aware of and responsive to each other's needs. We need this in marriage relationships, friendships, and especially child-parent relationships, as those early interactions set the foundation for future relationships.

This is why trauma in primary caregiving relationships causes such damage. Because when a baby learns from birth that his needs will not be acknowledged or responded to, he grows up with a sense of disharmony, an overwhelming feeling of being invisible to and out of sync with his world. This leads him to find his security through less effective means, such as emotional distance, obsessive control, or desperate codependence.

As adults, when you and I experience any kind of trauma or loss, we become that helpless child again. Our suffering forces us to face our mortality and our inability to control all circumstances. We realize, yet again, that the worst can happen and we can't do anything about it. When this happens, our healing requires emotional attunement, someone willing to see and respond to our needs, to acknowledge our circumstances and enter into them with us. Then and only then will we feel safe and start to heal.

It's often the routine of daily experiences in safe relationship with others that helps a person recover from the disastrous, unsafe experiences.

To be human is to wage a lifelong battle against our wounds and mortality, which means every one of us is fighting our own war. We may have the best intentions, but far too often we fail to offer attunement to those who most need it. Rather than offering safety, we attempt to secure our own through distance, detachment, control, or codependence. And rather than experiencing healing, we all end up a bit more broken.

We need a relationship that won't fail us, a bond that won't break. Someone willing and able to see our need and supply a resonating response to it. Someone able to feel our pain without succumbing to it.

And we have that someone in the incarnation.

While we're busy trying to escape mortality, God put it on. In response to our cries for relief, God put on flesh and blood, aches and pains, mood swings, exhaustion, and digestive distress. He left a pain-free existence of perfection, one without trauma or loss of any sort, and instead slipped each foot into the pant legs of the human predicament.

And He did it for one reason alone.

To be with us, to attune to us.

"For to us a child is born" (Isa. 9:6).

"The Word became *flesh* and made his dwelling *among us*. We have seen his glory, the glory of the one and only Son, who came from the Father, full of grace and truth" (John 1:14, emphasis mine).

"He was despised and rejected by mankind, a man of suffering, and familiar with pain. Like one from whom people hide their faces he was despised, and we held him in low esteem. Surely he took up our pain and bore our suffering" (Isa. 53:3–4).

The incarnation is the greatest miracle of all time. From birth to death, Jesus endured the full human experience. Aches and pains. Hunger. Sleepless nights. Disappointment. Weariness. Laughter. Delight. And yes, I'm pretty sure He barfed. That's part of the human experience too. The Sovereign, All-Powerful, All-Knowing One became a baby and did not exercise any of His rights.

Becoming one of us.

I've spent the last couple of years reading the Bible front to back. No timeline, no pressure, no rush. I'm reading it not for the notch in my belt but in the hope of maybe understanding it a little. This is at least the third time I've read the Bible through, and every time I do, I wrestle through the Old Testament. Although I savor the exodus story, Psalms, Isaiah, even Job's hard narrative, I struggle with the repeating theme of God's anger and the exacting of harsh consequences. One moment He speaks tenderly to His people, the next moment He's threatening to annihilate them.

I don't know how to reconcile the paradoxical nature of God. He is both terrifying and tender, righteous and compassionate, unapproachable and near. Often, I end up with a kink in my spiritual neck and a bad case of emotional whiplash. As much as I long to be close to my creator, I don't know how to connect emotionally with such an unpredictable God.

Until Jesus. God made tangible in the form of the vulnerable, wearing skin and carrying a beating heart the same as I do.

And suddenly the inaccessible God whose veiled presence hovered in a tabernacle moved out from behind the curtain to become someone I can see, touch, know. Whereas Dorothy's wizard proved a disappointment when the curtain was pulled back, Jesus proved to be a deliverer. Not less able to save us but even more.

God in the garden. God in a covenantal promise. God on a ladder reaching down from heaven. God in a pillar of cloud and a pillar of fire. God in a tabernacle. God in a whisper.

And now God in skin.

The relief brought by the incarnation is appreciated only after you and I have slogged through the pain and distance of the Old Testament. With each step, each chess move, God enters more deeply in. Moses is no longer the only one who can approach Him. The priests needn't offer blood to come near Him. God moves toward us, not away. His desire for nearness bridges the gap between holiness and humanity, righteousness and rebellion, to give us the one thing we most need.

Relationship.

And when I think of it this way, when I see the whole story and not only a small slice that's difficult to swallow, I can see how the severity of God's righteous wrath serves to make the severity of His relentless nearness more profound. Just as light is appreciated only by those who know the dark, it is the justice of His extreme anger that makes His extreme grace so compelling.

Only the most radical, extravagant, unquenchable love would cross such a distance to reach you. And to reach me.

"Since the children have flesh and blood, he too shared in their humanity so that by his death he might break the power of him who holds the power of death—that is, the devil—and free those who all their lives were held in slavery by their fear of death. For surely it is not angels he helps, but Abraham's descendants. For this reason he had to be made like them, *fully human in every way*, in order that he might become a merciful and faithful high priest in service to God" (Heb. 2:14–17, emphasis mine).

There are days I long to share space with someone who gets me. Someone who knows the struggle to swallow and eat, who understands my slip into self-consciousness when speaking in public, who knows the ongoing battle between faith and fear.

We have such a deep need to be understood, to know that other flesh-and-blood-wearers, especially those closest to us, understand our reality. And yet there's a disconnect. As well-meaning as most people may be, it is rare to find a person who sticks around long enough to empathize with our experience and bear it with us. It's easier to move on.

It's painful, for all of us. This deep aching desire to be known and understood, in all our pain and suffering, and yet our inability both to find people who get us and to become people who truly understand and empathize with others.

And yet there is one who does this without fail.

"Therefore, since we have a great high priest who has ascended into heaven, Jesus the Son of God, let us hold firmly to the faith we profess. For we do not have a high priest who is unable to empathize with our weaknesses, but we have one who has been tempted in every way, just as we are—yet he did not sin. Let us then approach God's throne of grace with confidence, so that we may receive mercy and find grace to help us in our time of need" (Heb. 4:14–16).

Atonement through attunement. Reparation of brokenness through an empathetic and redemptive response, the entering in of the incarnation, God Himself taking on our trauma so we can, finally, be whole.

•>◇<•

"Show me your scars," she said. "I'd really like to see them."

If anyone else had asked, the words might have felt awkward, intrusive. But this was Lindsey, my friend of several years whose body bore her own scars. More than a decade before, she'd nearly died in childbirth and slept forty-seven days in a coma, and she had spent the years since trying to recover. She knew how a scar could leave a girl in irreconcilable pieces.[31]

At the kindness of her question, my throat turned tight. I reached for my left shirtsleeve, rolled it up slowly, past wrist then elbow, to reveal the largest of my scars.

At least twelve inches, including a two-by-three-inch skin graft on the inside of my wrist. This is where they removed blood vessels and flesh to rebuild some semblance of a tongue. My left arm looked like a scene pulled from *Frankenstein*.

She reached her hand toward my arm. With a gentleness hard-earned, she touched the skin, her fingers tracing the long line of memory in the form of an ugly white scar.

I couldn't speak. She wouldn't. With a touch, I felt less alone. She entered in, sharing my pain. And a small part of my unseen wounds started to heal.

It has been more than three years since that day. I've thought of it many times, and her gesture has changed how I see and reach for other scarred people. Sometimes touch heals more than words, presence more than platitudes. And I now understand this is what God accomplished in the incarnation.

By becoming flesh and blood, God reached out a hand from the distance of heaven and touched humankind. Bridging the distance of holiness, He not only became someone we can touch but became the one reaching to touch us.

> "He touched her hand and the fever left her, and she got up and began to wait on him" (Matt. 8:15).

"He went in and took the girl by the hand, and she got up" (Matt. 9:25).

"But Jesus came and touched them. 'Get up,' he said. 'Don't be afraid'" (Matt. 17:7).

"Jesus had compassion on them and touched their eyes. Immediately they received their sight and followed him" (Matt. 20:34).

"After he took him aside, away from the crowd, Jesus put his fingers into the man's ears. Then he spit and touched the man's tongue" (Mark 7:33).

"Jesus reached out his hand and touched the man. 'I am willing,' he said. 'Be clean!' And immediately the leprosy left him" (Luke 5:13).

"Look at my hands and my feet. It is I myself! Touch me and see" (Luke 24:39).

In a world that pulled away from pain, Jesus pushed in. He reached for it, experiencing pain so we would know we're not alone in ours. What was once marked for death showed signs of new life.

Jesus—the flesh-and-blood presence of God with us—became the means to our atonement. The sacrifice cut in two, offered as payment for our breaking the sacred covenant. His death atones for the death we deserve.

But He is also our means of attunement. He will hold the basket while we barf, stay close while we suffer, and clean up our messes with His extravagant grace.

Show Me your scars, He urges.

Seeing our deepest needs, He doesn't pull back. Reaching with hands that bear their own wounds, He responds as no other human can or will.

He touches us at the place of our pain. Over and over again, with hands familiar with both suffering and healing.

Until we know, once again, we are not alone.

ALTAR STONE 7

LOOKING FOR GOD'S PRESENCE IN YOUR HUMANITY

The older I get, the more I find reason to gripe about my failing body. My eyes can't see, my joints ache, and my hair is losing color faster than a deck cushion in the hot summer sun. Pretty soon, it won't be gray; it'll be clear. But the truth is, I know firsthand the miracle of our working, functioning, life-giving bodies. Even those bodies that don't function like they're supposed to work a miracle every day they keep us alive. Take a moment to consider the flesh-to-flesh, flesh-to-creation interactions you've experienced. Eye contact, a smile shared. A friend who reached out with a needed hug or word of encouragement. The rose petals that felt like velvet in your hands. The warmth of the sun on the back of your neck. The comfort of a favorite blanket wrapping around your legs. The sound of a beautifully played composition. The human experience is rich with sensations. And each beautiful sensation testifies to the incarnation. Where have you seen evidence of God's presence in the human vulnerability of your story? Pray for God to open your eyes to see what you have missed. Then write it down. Mark it. This is your seventh altar stone.

I was living with my mom in a shack by the railroad track. The mining train stopped there on the way to and from the mine to get ore. As a child, I thought my mom was feeding the railmen lunch each day. They would come one by one around noon, and she would send me out to play. The railmen would let me ride on the caboose and help them switch the train track. I also got to sit in the engine . . . I was totally unaware that Mom was selling more than lunch to the miners . . . Almost all other memories of this period in my life seem lost in darkness and fear.

—DAD, DECEMBER 8, 2011

CHAPTER 8

A Prison

A GOD WHO IS WITH YOU IN YOUR DOUBT

> It is my ignorance of God's design that makes me quarrel with him.
>
> —JOHN FLAVEL, LATE MINISTER OF THE GOSPEL AT DARTMOUTH

It was my third trip to the airport in four days. And I had at least a half dozen more coming up in the days to follow.

The day after traveling home from a conference and doing a quick load of laundry, I drove back to the airport to pick up a colleague, Byron Emmert, and his wife, Linda. He and I were co-leading a communication conference that week in Colorado Springs.

As often happens with longtime friends, we quickly bypassed the chitchat and dove into the deep end of spiritual conversation. I was five months out from my second diagnosis of cancer and two months out from my dad's diagnosis of terminal pancreatic cancer. Although I was juggling more than a few emotions and questions, my faith held strong. It was to this subject that Byron directed his question.

"So how are you doing, really?"

I glanced at him in the passenger's seat. He looked at me with knowing eyes. Our long-standing friendship had earned him the right to ask honest questions. And require honest answers.

I don't remember exactly what I said. But I told him the truth as best I could: I trusted God's goodness and presence in the circumstances we understand as well as in those we don't. It was difficult to fathom why God would allow our family to deal with so much loss back to back. It seemed insensitive at best, callous at worst.

But I went on to mention the biblical story of John the Baptist and how his lack of understanding about his imprisonment had led him to wonder whether he'd had it wrong all along.

"I can't stop thinking about him," I told Byron and Linda. "He'd done everything right. He knew the Bible, followed it, made more sacrifices than most in his service to God. He even lived in the wilderness eating insects, for crying out loud."

I stared out the windshield, tried to understand what I'd contemplated many times.

"It just doesn't make sense," I continued. "Why didn't Jesus *do* something?"

For the rest of our drive, from Denver to Colorado Springs, we talked about God's sovereignty and wrestled with the apparent inconsistency of His intervention. And then how, as we sit in the prisons of our disappointment, we tend to question the reality of the God we've always loved. At the end of our drive, we parked in the venue parking lot and exited the car with our faith intact. With our confidence in God's presence and purposes still strong. Because our conversation centered on the theoretical, not the experiential.

I thought little of our conversation at the time. We faced the questions and overcame with faith. Surely that was the end of our trials.

I suspect the conversation was God's preparation. Because in the months following, the three of us faced circumstances that defied explanation and left us each breathless with the fight.

To begin, four weeks later, my father died of pancreatic cancer.

Two weeks after that, Linda had emergency surgery for a torn detached retina which resulted in extremely impaired vision in her left eye. Eight hours after Linda's surgery, Byron had a stroke in an optic nerve which resulted in blindness in his left eye.

Then, ten weeks after burying my dad, I found out I had cancer for the third time with no promise of a cure.

And the words we'd shared so casually that day in the car came back to haunt me. And to test me.

•➤◇➤•

If there's one verse my dad quoted more than any other while I was growing up, it was Galatians 6:7: "Do not be deceived: God cannot be mocked. A man reaps what he sows."

He usually wielded these words to curb any thought of disobedience, packaged with a stern look and a healthy dash of the fear of God. It worked. I was scared into submission, certain that if I made the smallest error, the God with the Great Big Seeing Eye would send down blazing consequences to purify me of my bad behavior.

On the upside, this saved me from the mistakes many of my peers stumbled into. I don't have any adolescent rebellion stories that fill my gut with regret.

On the downside, this fear-based obedience turned my interaction with God into something transactional. If I wanted a good life and unconditional love, I needed to do everything the Bible says—front to back. If I failed, any complications were my fault. Two plus two equals four, always.

Except when it doesn't. Sometimes the math doesn't work, and no one can explain why it doesn't.

This is what happened to John the Baptist.

Before birth, John had been marked as God's chosen forerunner to the Messiah, a town crier who would get the people ready for the coming King. Prophets like Isaiah (40:3–5) and Malachi (3:1; 4:5–6) foretold John's life and messianic significance hundreds of years before he took his first breath.

Then there was the matter of his miraculous birth. His parents,

Elizabeth and Zechariah, were both descendants of Aaron, of the tribe of Levi, Jacob's third son. Those in the tribe of Levi were set apart as priests of God, mediators between the people and God's presence in the temple. The same tribe of priests who carried the ark of the covenant across the Jordan River hundreds of years before.

One day, while Zechariah served as a priest in the temple, God appeared to him in a vision (Luke 1:5–25). In spite of his old age and his wife's barrenness, he and Elizabeth would have a son. And that child would be precursor to the Christ.

A connection between the people and God's promised salvation.

Knowing the significance of their son's life, Elizabeth and Zechariah raised him accordingly. When he was a young man, he went off to live in the wilderness, set apart for his sacred purpose. He called God's people to repent, to turn their hearts back to God, and he preached the good news to anyone who would listen (Matt. 3:1–12; Mark 1:1–8; Luke 3:1–20).

When Jesus was grown and ready to walk His hard road, He went to John to be baptized. John was the one to put his hands on Jesus, to lower Him and raise Him up again from the water. John saw the Spirit of God descend like a dove and land on Jesus, and he heard God's booming approval of His presence in the flesh of His only Son (Matt. 3:13–17; Luke 3:21–22).

The math was adding up.

Until, a short time later, King Herod threw John in prison (Luke 3:20). Angered by John's no-nonsense truth-telling about his illegitimate wife, Herodias, Herod locked him up, far removed from his wilderness preaching and the Messiah he'd spent a lifetime serving.

And in the dark basement of his dungeon, John's white-hot faith flickered.

Am I being punished?

Did I misread the signs?

I imagine he huddled on the filthy floor, both claustrophobic and cold after a lifetime in wide open spaces. Perhaps he ruminated over every word, rehearsed every decision, reexamined every step leading up to his predicament.

There must be an explanation. There has *to be a reason why.*

He needed reassurance, a black-and-white answer. I believe that's why he sent his closest friends to find Jesus and ask Him straight up.

"Are you the one who is to come, or should we expect someone else?" (Matt. 11:3).

You hear it, right? The shred of doubt. The ache for an answer to a prison-inspired question.

John's question does not surprise me. Some theologians believe John's question and errand were for his followers more than himself, that his faith was far too strong to experience doubt. And yet I know firsthand it doesn't take long in a dark prison to turn the staunchest faith upside down. Expectation is a possessive lover, likely to choke you when her needs aren't met.

While John's possible doubt makes me feel less alone in my own, I find the greatest comfort in Jesus' response.

"Go and tell John what you hear and see: the blind receive their sight and the lame walk, lepers are cleansed and the deaf hear, and the dead are raised up, and the poor have good news preached to them. And blessed is the one who is not offended by me" (Matt. 11:4–6 ESV).

Soon after John's message and Jesus' response, Jesus performed one of His greatest miracles: the feeding of the five thousand. An impressive miracle that appears in all four of the gospel accounts. And yet John ended up beheaded at Herod's command.

Five thousand strangers fed with a prayer. One close friend neglected and dead.

It's hard for me to understand, the seemingly random giving and withholding of miracles. Something in me stings with the injustice of it, perhaps because so many of my prayers remained unresolved. John had a need, and Jesus ignored it or, at the least, didn't do anything about it.

Blessed is the one who is not offended by Me, He said.

The NIV translates the word *offended* as "stumbles." The Amplified and NASB, "take offense." The NLB, "fall away." And TLB, "doubt." But the Greek word here is *skandalizo,* from which we get the word *scandalized.* One source describes the meaning as "a trap, stumbling block . . . To throw someone unawares into ruin."[32]

I read and reread Jesus' words and wrestled with the translations, trying to understand the intention of His words and the emotion of His heart. Although my doubts tried to drown out truth, I could almost hear a whisper in my ear.

Blessed is she whose faith is not ruined by Me.

In her book *Everything Happens for a Reason: And Other Lies I've Loved,* Kate Bowler shares her journey through a terminal cancer diagnosis at thirty-six years old. Nowadays, I can hardly stomach listening to anyone talk about suffering, because most do it from the protected distance of inexperience. Although well-intentioned, most sermons and explanations end up coming out trite and simplistic. And my experience with suffering has proved it to be neither. It's striking how easy it is to wax poetic about pain when we've experienced little of it ourselves.

But Kate Bowler is different.

She tells the ugly truth without toning it down or making it more palatable for the pious. She doesn't attempt to explain the unexplainable, nor does she turn tragedies trite. Instead, she faces disappointment, doubts, and disasters with raw emotion, frank truth-telling, wicked wit, and sharp insight.

"Control is a drug, and we are all hooked," Kate says.[33]

When I heard those words through my earbuds while on a morning run, I hit the back button so I could chew on the truth again. She's absolutely correct. We want to believe that disease, disaster, and tragedy can be prevented and avoided. That's why last week, for the umpteenth time, I received an unsolicited eight-page letter from a stranger detailing how I can cure myself of cancer. If only I would do this and avoid that and—this one stings the most—believe more. Behind the sender's pretense of help sits a poisonous implication: my suffering is my fault.

Not long ago, I spoke at a women's conference in Johannesburg, South Africa. For two days, I shared pieces of my story and how to build the kind of faith that stands up to the worst of life. During a break between sessions, a woman caught up with me as I headed to my seat to collect my notes. She beamed with abundant confidence.

"Oh, honey. Don't you worry." She patted my arm in reassurance. "God's not going to let you die. He has too much good work for you to do!"

Although she meant well, I knew her words weren't true.

It doesn't work that way. Just ask John the Baptist. And scores of other men and women through the centuries who served God faithfully and yet died prematurely. Some who will die even today.

Although I don't doubt the authenticity of my South African friend's faith, she'd developed a theory about life and death and God's role in both that gave her a sense of control. Just as an algebraic equation delivers an answer, God wouldn't let someone doing "good work" die. That meant that as long as she kept serving Him well, she had nothing to fear.

But God never made that guarantee. Jesus said quite the opposite: "In this world you will have trouble" (John 16:33).

I, too, have long been a control addict. I've known this, but I am only now starting to recognize how deep into the drug I am.

For a long time, I equated comfort with God's presence. Is life good? Then God is near. Is life hard, ugly, messy, brutal? Then God must be mad, distant, or indifferent. Bad circumstances can't exist in the presence of a good God unless I've done something wrong to deserve it.

As I said, control. I want a timeline of events and a play-by-play of God's interventions and responses, plan As, plan Bs, and a variety of contingencies. That way there are no sudden moves and grooves for which I'm unprepared.

But life and faith rarely work that way. Crises and conflicts occur without my consent. Then like a child who didn't get her way, I turn angry and indignant.

Like the Israelites who crafted lesser gods from wood and stone, I want a God small enough I can hold in my hands and carry in my pocket. I want to feel the whole of Him and see all the angles of Him. I retreat from the mystery and complexity and uncontainability of Him, afraid of what I don't understand.

Is God still with me, even here?

When I can't find answers to my questions, my faith hovers at the edge of ruin. And rather than a God big enough to rescue me, I end up with a pocket and a hand full of air.

Sometimes we're not ready for a word until we're ready for it.

The day was hot and the schedule full. I had more to accomplish than I had time to accomplish it. In spite of my dedicated Bible reading and attempts to pray, my soul felt dry, malnourished. God seemed distant, aloof, as if He'd grown weary of my vacillating emotions and weak faith and had found someone else to save.

I was a disappointment, I knew. And that alone made it hard to connect with a God who deserved better than I was giving Him.

Taking a break from work, I left my office and headed outside to clear my head and tackle a few weeds in my rock bed. Grabbing my iPod and headphones in an afterthought, I planned to listen to a book while pulling my rebellious adversaries out by the roots.

I pressed play and the book I'd started listening to a couple of weeks before picked up at the passage where I'd left off. You may call it coincidence, but I know better.

"For those who feel their lives are a grave disappointment to God, it requires enormous trust and reckless, raging confidence to accept that the love of Christ knows no shadow of alteration or change."

My breath caught. The words had been written by a flawed defunct priest more than two decades before, one who tried so hard to be good but ended up with his share of bad. A man by the name of Brennan Manning.

With a weed in my hand and the hot sun on my back, I could hardly move. His words were for me, I knew. I continued to listen.

"Just as the sunrise of faith requires the sunset of our former unbelief, so the dawn of trust requires letting go of our craving spiritual consolations and tangible reassurances. Trust at the mercy of the response it receives is a bogus trust. All is uncertainty and anxiety. In trembling insecurity, the disciple pleads for proofs from the Lord that her affection is returned. If she does not receive them, she is frustrated and starts to suspect that her relationship with Jesus is all over or that it never even existed."

I was the insecure disciple, pleading for proofs and unwilling to trust until I received them.

"If she does receive consolation, she is reassured, but only for a time. She presses for further proofs—each one less convincing than the one that went before. In the end the need to trust dies of pure frustration. What the disciple has not learned is that tangible reassurances, however valuable they may be, cannot create trust, sustain it, or guarantee any certainty of its presence. Jesus calls us to hand over our autonomous self in unshaken confidence. When the craving for reassurance is stifled, trust happens."[34]

Most people assume my biggest struggle through cancer and so many cumulative losses are the "why" questions. But that's not my tension. Suffering is universal, and I know I'm not exempt.

Rather, my obstacle is trust. I can read the words "God is love," but I can't quite make the leap to bank on it. I want reassurance that God's love is personal and He won't disappoint. That He will never stop showing up and that I'm worth coming after. Continuous, daily, tangible proofs.

But a lifetime of twisted theology led me to believe I am only as loved as my behavior is good. That weeds and disease are my fault, my responsibility. And that, unless I continue to perfect my performance and impress with my robust spirituality, God will tire of my failures and leave me in the dust.

This is the prison that can't be seen, not in bars and wardens and court documents declaring time served. Instead, it's a prison that rises up to ensnare us every time we doubt God's promise always to love and never to leave, every time we self-protect at the cost of trust.

It has been so hard for me to believe there is a love greater than those that have failed. A love that doesn't abuse, neglect, or run away but draws close. A love that, finally, heals the wounds I've been licking for too long.

"I will not leave you as orphans; I will come to you," Jesus said (John 14:18).

Every time I read those words I want to weep.

God won't always rescue me, that is true. But the Bible says He will always be with me. And the divide between the two is the distance between doubt and trust.

Frederick Buechner said, "If you don't have doubts you're either kidding yourself or asleep. Doubts are the ants-in-the-pants of faith. They keep it alive and moving."[35]

Ultimately, faith riddled with doubt forces me to choose. To choose between the visible and the invisible, the clarity and the mystery.

Will I trust Him based on His history? Or doubt Him based on my own? Can I huddle in John's prison and still believe the Jesus I've always known? Can I celebrate His obvious miracles even while mourning the lack of my own? Can I endure these moments of aloneness, these days when God feels so very far away, and still believe His promise never to leave me?

⁂

We are so infatuated with miracles. We pray for them, buy books about them, search far and near for one of our own. We even entice God to respond by making sweeping promises and attempting to manipulate His affection.

I imagine we think a miracle will solidify our faith, provide proof that what we believe isn't unfounded. Besides, there is certainly nothing wrong with praying for a miracle, believing in a miracle, and then celebrating it if and when it comes. Our God is the God of the impossible.

The Bible is filled with examples of these kinds of praying-believing-receiving miracles. I've experienced a few inexplicable moments myself. And although His deliverance rarely happens like I expect, it takes my breath away.

But we mustn't forget: The disciples saw three years of back-to-back miracles. The sick healed. The dead revived. Jesus silenced storms, fed thousands, cast out demons, touched outcasts, and rescued the rebellious. But when the bottom fell out in a late-night garden arrest, every single one of those who claimed to love Him left Him. Applause and adoration turned to running shoes and doubt. As pastor Leonard Sweet said recently, "Jesus is mystery, not equation. Add him up, you still don't have it. Jesus didn't come to earth so we could use him as 'proof' or to prove a point. He is the point, and the church has often missed the point when it forgets this."[36]

Miracles don't always make faith. Tangible proofs don't guarantee trust. Suffering, loss, difficulty, questions, wrestling, and the oceanic grace and unflinching presence of God do. And, perhaps, the fact that grace and nearness show up in those kinds of places is, in spite of us, the real miracle. Then, as St. Augustine said, "if we but turn to God, that itself is a gift of God."[37]

Blessed is the one who is not ruined by Me but who trusts Me, even there.

When I first dreamed the concept for this book, I set out to deliver evidences of God's presence. Definitive proof. A collection of feel-good stories, armed with theological proof, that would buoy our faith. If I strip away all pseudospirituality, however, I'd have to admit that lurking behind my spiritual study was a fantasy of fireworks. I wanted inexplicable rescues, divine interventions, glorious displays of God's strength and healing and power.

I wanted a Hollywood God. In the presence of such incontrovertible, wood-and-stone evidence, I would know that God is real, good, and with us. I suspected the sensational would ease the discomfort of the unexplained.

Instead, God called my bluff. Didn't respond to my invitations to show up and show off. Instead, He left me to choose in whom and what I would believe.

The evidence He's provided from Genesis 1 to Revelation 22 is already enough. And the only thing revealed by my attempts to entice divine spiritual fireworks was my inability to trust.

Perhaps our greatest prison isn't the pain we suffer in our incarcerations but our lagging ability to trust while sitting in them. The way we cling to our control rather than surrender to the not-knowing, not-understanding, not-resolving. We are—I am—so very desperate for explanations, reasons, something or someone to tell us how we ended up where we are. We think the answers will bring light to our darkness, set us free of our prisons.

Perhaps they might, temporarily. But sooner or later, we will once again land in a circumstance outside the reach of our lamps. Then all the reasons that felt bright enough in the first crisis won't light up the second.

What we need is not more proof of Him but more trust in Him.

"Where there is true faith, yet there may be a mixture of unbelief," a seventeenth-century Welsh minister, Matthew Henry, said. "The Old-Testament prophets were sent mostly to kings and princes, but Christ preached to the congregations of the poor."[38]

This is good news for the likes of you and me. We, the shabby, worn-down company of the poor. Those of us who believe and yet doubt. Those whose stomachs growl for a feast of faith and yet can scrounge up only a couple of pennies of trust.

Perhaps it's time to revisit the miracles and evidences we've already seen. He has doggedly pursued us in spite of our every attempt to push Him out. His presence is big enough to enter into the dark places, confusing places, ugly and beyond-understanding places and, by the sheer magnitude of His mystery, shine a light far too bright to be eclipsed by our doubt.

If I dare trust Him even here, doubt turns out to be a gift. A strange, hard gift, to be sure. But the means of a deeper faith. And if faith grows in a darkness with every sinister attempt to ruin it, then perhaps that is the real miracle after all.

ALTAR STONE 8

LOOKING FOR GOD'S PRESENCE IN YOUR DOUBT

Doubt can be some of the most fertile ground for deepening and strengthening your faith. Rather than assume shame or guilt as a result of your questions, pay attention to them and allow them to drive you deeper into the depths of Scripture and closer to the heart of God. Doubt is dangerous only when it stops seeking the truth. Consider the questions and doubts that plague your faith. What is niggling you? What causes you worry or fear or makes you question the reality of God? How might God be showing you an aspect of His presence in your prison? Pray for God to open your eyes to see what you have missed. Then write it down. Mark it. This is your eighth altar stone.

During the summer [before my fourth grade year], Mom offered me a bicycle if I would come to live with her. Dad told me he wouldn't buy me a bike, so I left with her. That horrific time lasted until I entered sixth grade. Mom was living with a retired army master sergeant named Jim. He clearly didn't like me . . . Each morning, he'd wake me up very early by tapping my forehead with his army .44 caliber pistol loaded and cocked. I had to jump up and do pushups until he told me I could quit. He would whip me with the same pistol if he didn't like how low I was wearing my pants or how I combed my hair. This was an almost daily ritual.

—DAD, DECEMBER 8, 2011

CHAPTER 9

A Transfiguration

A GOD WHO IS WITH YOU IN YOUR TRANSFORMATION

Someone I loved once gave me
a box full of darkness.

It took me years to understand
that this, too, was a gift.

—MARY OLIVER, "THE USES OF SORROW"

In my deepest wound I saw your glory, and it dazzled me.

—AUGUSTINE OF HIPPO

We sat inches apart on the couch, watching the season opener of the National Football League's Denver Broncos.

"If I could go back in time, I'd be a sports commentator," I announced. This did not surprise him. After nearly two decades of marriage, my husband had heard me make this declaration many times before.

"And"—I shifted to sit a bit taller—"I'll have you know I would've been the *best* female commentator the National Football

League had ever seen." My voice grew stronger with each word, culminating in one final pronouncement: "Ever!"

He'd heard this routine before.

My love of sports—NFL football in particular—began in the 1970s on a sectional sofa in my parents' family room. For six months of the year, my childhood Sundays were marked by church in the morning and evening, with NFL football sandwiched in between. My dad was a die-hard Dallas Cowboys fan, meaning I cut my teeth watching Tom Landry coach his Cowboys to victory along with star players like Roger Staubach, Tony Dorsett, and Herschel Walker.

Several years after our family moved from Arizona to Illinois, the Chicago Bears started their rise to the top. Then came the mid-1980s with coach Mike Ditka and star players like Jim McMahon, Walter "Sweetness" Payton, and William "The Refrigerator" Perry. We caught the fever. Dallas may have still been our live-or-die-for team, but we couldn't help but tap our feet to the "Super Bowl Shuffle" and cheer for "da Bearssss" with the rest of their fans. (If none of this rings a bell, google it, you crazy whippersnapper, you.)

By the time I graduated high school, I understood the positions, the plays, and what it takes to have a winning football team. My NFL obsession continued into adulthood, although my team changed when I moved to Denver, Colorado. Turns out the move was well timed, because that was the first of two consecutive years that John Elway's Broncos took the Super Bowl. A fine time to become a Broncos fan, and I have been one ever since.

Of course, seasons of failures often follow seasons of success, which is what happened with the Broncos. I'd prefer to bury those years of pain and suffering until 2012, when Peyton Manning came on the scene.

Even so, I know this is how it works; life is more a rhythm than a trajectory. It's what I call a both-and scenario. Successes *and* failures. Improvements *and* setbacks. Wins *and* losses.

Both-and. Not either-or.

To be loyal to the relationship, fans need to learn how to create space for the tension.

My shameless bragging on the couch lasted no more than a minute. Then, like a deflating balloon, I let out a sigh that came all the way from my toes. My husband recognized that too.

I missed my voice. My precancer, presurgery voice. The voice that had been central to my career and ministry, that had earned an income and made me feel connected with my purpose. The voice that had sounded good on radio and television and didn't make listeners cringe. And the voice that could have, if I'd put my mind to it, made my broadcasting, sports-commentating dreams come true.

But that dream, as well as so many others, died the day cancer stole my tongue. The world doesn't have room for the broken and disfigured. A woman with flawed speech has no place on public television or a radio program or a podcast. Either-or, not both-and.

This is what I believed. And there wasn't a darn thing I could do about it.

Most of my friends find it strange that a girl like me boasts of such a love of football and sports. I can't explain it really, except for this:

First, sports teach me a lot about leadership and life. There's something about diverse people with various stories and talents coming together with a common goal that inspires me. I love the teamwork, the conflict, the strategy, the last-minute comebacks, and especially the shining smile of an underdog who surprises the world with a win. The overcoming gets me every time.

But I also watch football because it reminds me of Sunday afternoons on the couch with my dad. Although he usually ended up snoring before halftime, faith and football were the threads that connected us, the two things we agreed on and could talk about for hours. We may have gotten many things wrong, but we somehow managed to get those two things right. On Sundays, in spite of the tension between us, we experienced the best of each other, when Jesus and the NFL bridged the divide and brought us together.

Both-and.

In his classic book *Changes That Heal,* Dr. Henry Cloud shares what he believes are the four necessary developmental milestones we need to reach to function well in our day-to-day lives. God Himself demonstrates these qualities. So if we want to reflect His image and experience transformation, we must learn how to grow in these skills ourselves.

These "changes that heal" include the ability to (1) bond with others, (2) separate from others, (3) sort out issues of good and bad, and (4) take charge as an adult.[39]

If only it were so clear and simple in practice. I found Cloud's wisdom insightful and timely, although I wish someone would've held me down and made me read it back in 1992 when it first released. I could have saved myself (and my loved ones) many years of unnecessary pain and suffering. Of the nearly three hundred pages of rich insight, the foundational concept that stopped me in my tracks showed up in the first twenty-five pages:

> Grace and truth together reverse the facts of the fall, which were separation from God and others. Grace and truth together invite us out of isolation and into relationship. Grace, when it is combined with truth, invites *the true self,* the "me" as I really am, warts and all, into *relationship.* It is one thing to have safety in relationship; it is quite another to be truly known and accepted in this relationship.
>
> With grace alone, we are safe from condemnation, but we cannot experience true intimacy. When the one who offers grace also offers truth (truth about who we are, truth about who he or

> she is, and truth about the world around us), and we respond with our true self, then real intimacy is possible. Real intimacy always comes in the company of truth.[40]

I read those lines for the first time about six months ago. Immediately, I highlighted them in neon blue marker, making extra notations around five words: "then real intimacy is possible."

Since that day, I've reread the lines at least a dozen times, shared them with multiple close friends, and once read them out loud to a group of women leaders I mentor, provoking their oohs and aahs.

The reason for the resonance sits in our DNA. Humankind longs for intimacy, connection with a significant other. Although the degree to which we desire this may be impacted by personality and history, connection is essential to our survival.

But this need is compromised by the fact that we tend to divide ourselves into grace and truth camps. Because we can't seem to marry the two, we assume it can't be done. As a result, we choose one or the other as the answer to all of our problems. Either-or rather than both-and.

But in the New Testament, the disciple John alters this partisan perception by introducing the incarnation in a revolutionary way: "The Word became flesh and *made his dwelling among us.* We have seen his glory, the glory of the one and only Son, who came from the Father, *full of grace and truth*" (John 1:14, emphasis mine).

Grace *and* truth. Not either-or but both-and.

Whereas God's Old Testament presence took the form of truth—the Law and the Prophets—God's New Testament presence took the form of grace—Jesus. This is the gospel. But the real Good News is that rather than replacing truth, Jesus' grace completed it (Matt. 5:17). As Andy Stanley writes, "If the law were a homework assignment, He was completing it. If the law were a speech, He was concluding it. If the law were a plane, He was landing it."[41] Jesus embodied the perfect harmony of this paradox. Whereas truth shines a white-hot light on our sin and distance from God, grace reaches out a hand, touches us, and pulls us into relationship with Him.

Unfortunately, you and I don't live out that harmony nearly as well. Instead, we err on one side or the other.

We become licentious in our softness, using the grace of God as a get-out-of-jail-free card and as justification of a hedonistic life. We hurt ourselves and each other while ignoring the corrective sting of regret and guilt, both of which are necessary for developing character and maturity.

Or we become legalistic in our worship of truth. We're critical, blunt, harsh in our correction of society and individuals, feeling it our duty to point out every flaw, every misstep, every compromise of righteousness with a flaming tongue and the withdrawal of relationship. We stand guard at the back of our churches, making sure no one gets in who doesn't deserve to be there, assuming we alone know the standard.

But to embrace either grace or truth without the other is immaturity and slavery. It is only when they come together that the game of life boasts no underdog. For grace to leave its beautiful mark, truth needs to be respected, valued, and understood. And for truth to bring light and healing, there must be a net of grace to catch every one of us who gets caught with our pants down in its glare.

None of us can stand upright in the presence of truth. But none of us is beyond grace's ability to lift us back to our feet again.

Only God brings grace and truth together in perfect rhythm and harmony. The rest of us may attempt to follow His lead and do the same, but we will never get the composition right.

But the grace and truth of God are sufficient for that too. These two qualities of God's character sit solidly under the changes that promise to heal us, restore us. And knowing we'd struggle to make sense of these paradoxical aspects of His nature, God provided a poignant picture to make sure we'd never forget.

When Jesus invited three of His twelve disciples to join Him on an exclusive hike up a mountain, I bet they had no idea they were about to witness a spectacular meeting of heaven and earth.

The three synoptic gospels tell the story—Matthew, Mark, and Luke. According to Matthew 17:1, Jesus led Peter, James, and John "up a high mountain by themselves." When they arrived at their destination, suddenly "he was transfigured before them" (17:2). The Greek word used for "transfigured" is important, because it's the root from which we get our word *metamorphosis*. He wasn't changed in appearance only; he was transformed. Like a caterpillar providing a sneak peek of his winged future, God revealed the divine nature residing behind Jesus' veil of human flesh. Why? So Peter, James, and John could see who He'd been all along.

God. The I AM.

Fully human. And fully divine. Both-and.

To help us mortals get an idea of what that looked like to human eyes, Matthew said His face "shone like the sun, and his clothes became as white as the light" (17:2). As a mama who does her share of laundry, I appreciate Mark's note that Jesus' clothes became "whiter than anyone in the world could bleach them" (9:3). And Luke, the detailed physician, made sure we knew Jesus was praying when "the appearance of his face changed, and his clothes became as bright as a flash of lightning" (9:29).

This was no accident, this mountaintop display of divine glory to three men who would soon lead the new church. Jesus knew they struggled to comprehend His identity, that they didn't yet grasp Jesus' primary purpose and the difficult road He would soon walk.

Two more figures then joined Jesus on the mountain: Moses and Elijah. Moses represented the covenant and the Ten Commandments—the law. And Elijah represented the prophets, the brave men and women who fearlessly delivered God's words to God's people, in spite of the persecution and death threats they suffered as a result. This wasn't the first time Moses and Elijah stood on a mountain in God's presence. (See chapters 5 and 6.) But this time they witnessed the fulfillment of what their cave experiences had only hinted of.

Now it's our turn to bear witness. You see what's happening on the top of that mountain, don't you? Moses, Elijah, and Jesus. Together, shooting the breeze and snacking on some trail mix. The first two representing truth. And the last representing grace.

Both-and.

Jesus. God *and* man. Truth *and* grace.

Peter, James, and John were equal to them in number but no match for divine glory. Terrified at the supernatural display, Peter offered to build three shelters, or "tabernacles," to house Moses, Elijah, and Jesus. As an Israelite who grew up with tabernacles and temples, this made sense to him. He didn't yet realize that God's glory could not be contained. This was a moment not to perform a service but to worship a presence.

"This is my Son, whom I love; with him I am well pleased. Listen to him!" (Matt. 17:5).

That's when God the Father spoke, and I imagine those last three words exploded like thunder from heaven, shaking the earth. Which explains why Peter, James, and John found themselves facedown on the ground, paralyzed with fear.

Truth does that. It has a way of putting each one of us in the dirt. But just as quickly, the hand of grace lifted them up.

"But Jesus came and touched them. 'Get up,' he said. 'Don't be afraid'" (v. 7).

Grace does that. It has a way of lifting up those who least deserve it.

Then, almost as fast as the revelation showed itself, it disappeared. Moses and Elijah were gone. Jesus remained, but looking much like the ordinary man they'd left fishing nets to follow. And the glory they'd witnessed moments before faded.

⋄

I've often thought that if only I could experience a mountaintop transfiguration—or a hospital visitation—I would be able to believe without doubt. If the veil between heaven and earth lifted, my faith would no longer be susceptible to catastrophe or crisis.

I assume a mountaintop experience would provide a solid footing. And would make the forty years of wilderness-walking and faith-doubting a distant memory.

> On Christ the solid rock I stand,
> all other ground is sinking sand,
> all other ground is sinking sand.[42]

But then I read Jesus' words before and after the transfiguration. Matthew, Mark, and Luke all place the mountaintop experience smack dab in the middle of the first two of Jesus' morbid announcements about His impending death:

> "The Son of Man must suffer many things and be rejected by the elders, the chief priests and the teachers of the law, and he must be killed and on the third day be raised to life" (Luke 9:22).
>
> "Listen carefully to what I am about to tell you: The Son of Man is going to be delivered into the hands of men" (Luke 9:44).

Twenty-two verses and a transfiguration apart, Jesus wanted the disciples—and all of us—to know the point isn't what happened on top of the mountain. The real glory is in the willing descent to the bottom.

And if they wanted to follow Him, they'd need to live for more than the mountaintop moments too.

"Then he said to them all: 'Whoever wants to be my disciple must deny themselves and take up their cross daily and follow me. For whoever wants to save their life will lose it, but whoever loses their life for me will save it. What good is it for someone to gain the whole world, and yet lose or forfeit their very self?" (Luke 9:23–25).

The following day, the four—Jesus, Peter, James, and John—came back down the mountain (Luke 9:37). A crowd of followers and fans waited for them with diseases that needed healing and hearts that needed tending. Caught up in the energy of ministry, it didn't take long for the disciples to forget Moses, Elijah, and a mountaintop transfiguration.

Instead, they began arguing about who was the greatest in the kingdom, each one vying for the position of greatest importance. They didn't get it, just as we don't. Even so, Jesus didn't hide the truth. He kept telling them, even if they didn't yet understand.

> "For it is the one who is least among you all who is the greatest" (Luke 9:48).
>
> "Foxes have dens and birds have nests, but the Son of Man has no place to lay his head" (Luke 9:58).
>
> "Woe to you Pharisees, because you love the most important seats . . . and respectful greetings" (Luke 11:43).
>
> "And you experts in the law . . . because you load people down with burdens they can hardly carry, and you yourselves will not lift one finger to help them" (Luke 11:46).
>
> "If anyone comes to me and does not hate father and mother, wife and children, brothers and sisters—yes, even their

> own life—such a person cannot be my disciple" (Luke 14:26–27).

"Will you really lay down your life for me?" (John 13:38).

They wanted the glory. But Jesus' road to glory was paved with poverty. At the bottom of the mountain, not the top of it.

This is our struggle. It is when the glory fades to a dream we can't quite remember, when the loved one dies and the disease returns, when a job ends and the bills remain unpaid, when parents fail and churches wound and relationships remain unreconciled, that we forget what we once witnessed. The mountaintop experience doesn't last as long as we think it does.

That's the truth. And yet grace finds us, even there.

⁂

Very little is said about Jesus' human appearance in the Bible. Artists have attempted renderings of Him for centuries. And yet I suspect not one of them has produced anything close to a true representation.

But this I know: we paint Him as far more beautiful than He was.

"He grew up before him like a tender shoot, and like a root out of dry ground. He had no beauty or majesty to attract us to him, nothing in his appearance that we should desire him" (Isa. 53:2).

No beauty, nothing desirable. What the world deems attractive, He did not possess. He was ordinary and not worth a second glance or a bathroom-mirror selfie.

I've read these words from Isaiah dozens of times over the years. But it wasn't until my own body and appearance suffered that I appreciated them. From a distance, I don't look unusual or different. To friends and family who've known me my whole life, the changes are noticeable, but inconsequential.

But to the woman who has stared at the same face and body

in the mirror for four decades, the changes glare. I see the spidering burn scars covering my chest and circling around my neck. I see the quarter-sized scar where the tracheostomy allowed me to breathe and saved my life. I see the long, white, six-inch slice that follows ear to chin along the left side of my neck where the surgeons removed lymph nodes and my submandibular gland.

And then there are the flaws no one else sees. The second belly button where my feeding tube kept me alive. The fake tongue made of tissue from my arm and thigh that allows me to eat and drink but keeps me from properly kissing my husband. And the internal, biological, and systemic changes that cause my body to perform far less efficiently than before because of the poisons that dripped through a needle in my arm and infiltrated every cell in my body.

Mine is now a life of disability and disfigurement. Not extreme, but enough to make day-to-day life complicated and, at times, isolating. It is difficult to live in a body that no longer works, especially when you'd lived with one that did for so long. Although my struggles and scars are far less significant than some, I've developed a new empathy for those who look different, speak different, and for those who feel excluded and outside the reach of ordinary life. We are not always welcoming to those who are different.

This makes me consider how my dad's trauma disfigured him. It may not have shown up in white scars and skin grafts, but it marked him just the same. His need for safety at times looked like control, anger, and criticism. But behind these superficial expressions sat a deeper, more painful wound: the scar of abandonment and abuse.

My one comfort is the fact that Jesus understood this.

"There were many who were appalled at him—his appearance was so disfigured beyond that of any human being and his form marred beyond human likeness" (Isa. 52:14).

He was transfigured and disfigured. The same thirty-three-year-old God-man who experienced mountaintop transfiguration also experienced Golgotha disfiguration.

To disfigure is "to impair (as in beauty) by deep and persistent injuries"[43] or "to spoil the appearance of someone or something; to damage, mark."[44]

This sums up Jesus' experience. But it also sums up mine. My dad's. My children's. And yours. Deep and persistent injuries—physical, spiritual, and emotional, collected over a lifetime—have altered us, marked us. When we look in the mirror, it's not difficult to see disfigurement, inside and out.

And yet the transfiguration also helps me to see that sometimes our flesh veils what God is accomplishing within. To transfigure means "to change the appearance of someone or something, especially in a way that makes them beautiful. To give a new and typically exalted or spiritual appearance; to transform outwardly and usually for the better."[45]

The Latin root of both words—disfigure and transfigure—is *figurare*. And it simply means "to shape, fashion."[46]

Jesus' presence with us, His dirt-level, poverty-paved road to His death, showed us that what man can disfigure, God can transfigure. God's presence with us lifts the scar-torn veil of our human experience and reshapes and fashions us into something reflecting divine glory.

Disfigured *and* transfigured. Both-and.

It is our scars that make the beauty of His shaping that much more profound. Truth *and* grace. This is the painful and beautiful paradox of our human experience, that we can be so very broken (truth) and so very beautiful (grace). Capable of terrible evil and yet rescued by an extravagant love.

And for the little girl and her father sitting on the couch together watching Sunday football, the ability to hold this tension bridges the divide and brings them together.

We can be so very scarred and disfigured, nursing valid wounds of a human race gone awry. And yet we can, somehow, learn to sit together on the same couch of grace, God's presence transfiguring into glory what had once torn us apart.

ALTAR STONE 9

LOOKING FOR GOD'S PRESENCE IN YOUR TRANSFORMATION

The only way to see growth is to keep an eye on it over time. Every day when I look at my youngest three children, I don't see their legs growing or arms lengthening. But when I put them up to a wall and pencil their progress over years, I see significant evidence of how they've grown and changed. The same is true for our spiritual growth. How are you different than you were twenty years ago, ten years ago, one year ago? Take a keen look at the road you've walked and the ways you've become a better man or woman as the result of God's grace and truth in your life, during the experiences on the mountaintop and the tough descent down from it. You may feel a bit banged up and bruised from the journey, but God is able to transfigure what has been disfigured. Pray for God to open your eyes to see what you have missed. Then write it down. Mark it. This is your ninth altar stone.

I learned . . . that there were consequences to my actions—to my choices. I was lonely . . . I didn't like me . . . During one of my dad's drunken spells, he told me, "Punky, people like you until they get to know you and then they hate you." For most of my childhood and teen years, I bought into this devastating evaluation of myself and lived as if it was true.

—DAD, DECEMBER 8, 2011

CHAPTER 10

A MEAL

A GOD WHO IS WITH YOU IN YOUR HUNGER

One thing Jesus did in the Eucharist was to connect, in a vivid and simple way, eating with obedience and worship. He joined earth with heaven, bread with manna, flesh with Spirit. He linked physical hunger with spiritual hunger. He reminded us that every bite is also a prayer.

—MARK BUCHANAN, *THE REST OF GOD*

The world is perishing for lack of the knowledge of God and the Church is famishing for want of His Presence.

—A. W. TOZER, *THE PURSUIT OF GOD*

My soul shall be satisfied as with marrow and fatness; and my mouth shall praise thee with joyful lips: when I remember thee upon my bed, and meditate on thee in the night watches.

—PSALM 63:5–6 KJV

There are starving children in Africa."

Dad would not be messed with. We knew this. To refuse to eat the dinner Mom prepared was not an option, even if it looked like alien excrement from *Guardians of the Galaxy.*

I might exaggerate. Truth is my mom was and is an amazing cook, and I could fill a solid page detailing dishes she serves up to friends and family alike. But back in the 1970s and '80s, canned beets, marinated cabbage, and steamed brussels sprouts that turned to paste on contact were a tough sell to our pint-sized selves.

"They would be grateful to have that food sitting in front of you," Dad added with a disapproving glare, hoping the fear and guilt would sway our obedience.

I once innocently offered to box it up and send it to the starving children. Once.

Dad's motivational strategies worked. I was too scared of him and sad for faceless starving babies to disobey. I choked down my brussels paste, even if I ended up a bit green in the process. My brother, on the other hand, guzzled a gallon of water during those dinners, using the liquid as a vehicle to carry the food past his tastebuds. Brilliant.

By the time we excused ourselves from the table, I was nauseated and he sloshed when he walked.

At times Dad would add to the starving children narrative tales of his own childhood drama. Like the time his mom took off for days and didn't come home, leaving her two smallest children alone with only a few old onions and a bottle of mustard to eat.

"We had mustard and onion sandwiches for a week," he told us.

But we were too young to get it. To a child, his stories of hardship were fictional legends, along the lines of stories of parents who walked ten miles to school without shoes, in snow up to their armpits, both ways, on one leg, in the dark while being pursued by rabid animals. Without proof, it was hard to believe him.

Now, so many years later, I see the evidence I'd missed. Tiny signs that, when added up, pointed to Dad's hunger.

The way he ate his dinner as if it were a race, finishing long before the rest of us started.

The almost obsessive scraping of the remnants of food off his plate, and the way he'd sop up any juice with a piece of bread to make sure none of it was wasted. We often joked that Dad's was the only plate that didn't need a trip through the dishwasher.

And his meticulous devouring of apples and chicken legs, leaving nothing but seeds and bones. Sometimes he even swallowed the seeds and sucked the marrow out of the bones.

And in his later years, when his income could support it, the way he dined at restaurants, sometimes three times a day, so that he could be filled to the gills with plates full of rich food.

Only now can I see the message these proofs tried to tell me about my father.

It wasn't about the food.

It was about the hunger. His desperation to finally be filled.

One of the most difficult aspects of living an integrated, connected life in the absence of a normal tongue is the ritual of eating three times a day. What was once a source of nourishment and enjoyment has become a frustrating and often painful chore.

It's not just the mechanics of it, although that part is quite complicated. Two-thirds of my tongue is built from tissue and vessels taken from my neck and left forearm. The surgeons shaped that tissue like a flap around the remaining portion of my tongue, then tethered it to the base of my mouth. This means it doesn't move and groove like yours does. Imagine trying to eat with a gym sock in your mouth. Puts a damper on things.

But more than the difficult mechanics, I've lost much of the enjoyment of eating. The majority of my tongue lacks tastebuds. And the few that remain were burned by radiation. In addition, surgery severed a nerve. Add all that up, and according to the doctor's best estimate, I probably have somewhere between 20 and 30 percent of my ability to taste left.

I don't recommend it.

We don't appreciate our physiology's fine-tuning until something happens to shake it up. We overlook so much of the miracle of daily life until we lose it.

For the most part, I do okay when I'm alone. I don't have to worry about manners, and I don't have to navigate the conversation that accompanies a meal shared with others.

But more often than not, eating happens in community. And I can't eat and talk at the same time.

During a typical meal, you take a bite of food, chew it, swallow it, and then make small talk, possibly grab a quick sip of water. Maybe you ask your wife about her day or check in with your children about school. If you're supping with colleagues from work or friends from church, you may discuss an important project or ask them about a recent holiday or family adventure.

Sharing a meal is much like the Colorado Symphony performing Tchaikovsky. With a single composer and music selection guiding them, the various instruments alternately play solos as well as accompaniment. When the clarinets are done, the strings take over, then the percussion or brass. Music is a give-and-take of the various players and parts, and the result of the corporate participation is a harmonious experience that hints of the divine.

The problem for me is that I can no longer play my instrument with precision. I can no longer keep the same rhythm and timing as everyone else sitting at the table. For me, eating takes an extraordinary amount of time and focus. If I move too quickly, I choke or injure myself. I need to swallow multiple times for every bite of food to go down. That means if someone asks me a question, it might be several minutes before my mouth is available to answer it. Most people tire of waiting. And when a dinner conversation turns to a topic that interests me, I can't chew and swallow fast enough to join in. By the time I'm able to speak, the rest of the symphony has moved on to a different piece of music.

At each meal, I'm required to choose. Connect and converse? Or chew and swallow? I can satisfy either my hunger for food or my hunger for human connection. But I cannot do both.

I've learned to navigate this with family and close friends. They don't mind when wayward lettuce flies across the room while I'm answering a question, and they pretend they don't notice when I launch ground beef while laughing at a story. I may eat like a toddler, but they love me enough to overlook it.

For me, it remains humiliating. And isolating. To expose my vulnerability in these moments feels like opening the old underwear drawer for a group of strangers. It's raw, vulnerable, embarrassing. How do I lay the worst part of myself out on the table in the presence of others? At times, the gamble is too great.

You may not realize it, but a dinner table isn't really about the food.

It's about the people. And the relationships that are built three times a day at its altar.

Sharing a table is a sharing of our humanity and our common need for nourishment, day after day, to survive. But that requires trust. And safety. Only then, as we fork roast and potatoes into our mouths, regardless of how long it takes us to chew and to swallow, we might find a way to solve the deeper hunger that plagues each one of us.

⁂

In 1495, the heart of the Renaissance, Leonardo da Vinci began a work that became one of the most significant artistic productions in all of history: *The Last Supper.*

Displayed on the dining room wall of the Santa Maria delle Grazie monastery in Milan, Italy, *The Last Supper* is da Vinci's interpretation of the gospel account of Jesus' last supper with His disciples. In his painting, he captures the moment Jesus tells His closest friends that one of them will betray Him. The table is covered with all the evidence of a shared meal and familiar companionship. But their faces reflect nothing but shock and disbelief at Jesus' announcement.

A betrayal? And by one of the inner circle?! Inconceivable.

Most Renaissance masters painted their frescos on wet plaster, mixing their paint with the wet material. Leonardo da Vinci, however, had no experience with this type of mural art. He painted directly onto the dry plaster wall, and within decades the paint started to flake and peel.

In the hundreds of years since, numerous meticulous restorations have been performed to recapture the colors as closely as possible to da Vinci's original and to provide us with the mural we can buy tickets to see close-up. But the truth is that very little of da Vinci's work—if any—is left. It's been lost to time, covered by generations of well-meaning artists and admirers.[47] Even so, it remains beautiful and worth contemplation.

The biblical Last Supper is one of the few New Testament stories that appears in all four gospels—Matthew, Mark, Luke, and John. This speaks to its significance and the impact it had on those who shared it.

Today I sat down and read all four accounts, comparing the varying details and nuances of each. At the same time, I gazed at an online image of da Vinci's rendition of the Last Supper, allowing the art to trigger my imagination.

Meals matter to me. Especially final meals that happen right before a life-altering event. I still remember my "last supper," the night before the surgery to remove my tongue. Tri-tip steak, seasoned and cooked tender until it fell apart, homemade hand-cut egg noodles (my mama's recipe), mashed potatoes with extra butter, and sweet corn. Delish.

Final meals are rich with significance, full of the flavor of what is and what is yet to come. But to understand this particular meal and its implications, we need to understand the historical context.

Although table sharing has a modicum of significance in our modern context, it played a central role in ancient cultures. Hundreds and thousands of years ago, people had extremely limited social entertainment. So sharing a meal around a table played a much more important role in community life.

For the people of Israel, in particular, meals involved the observance of clear boundaries, differentiating God's people from the rest of the world. According to Old Testament law, Israelites were to remain separate, dining only with fellow Jews. Moreover, to share a meal with someone was to accept them as part of your family. In a sense, you were telling your guest that you trusted them enough to join your families in marriage.[48]

The meal wasn't about food. It was about intimacy. And an invitation to a committed familial relationship.

This is why the Pharisees of Jesus' day exploded in anger when Jesus ate dinner with politicians, prostitutes, the sick and mentally ill. "I must stay at your house today," Jesus told the thief Zacchaeus, an announcement that spit in the faces of the rule-following religious leaders (Luke 19:5). God had set the boundaries; why wasn't Jesus respecting them? He was crossing lines that weren't meant to be crossed.

What they failed to grasp? Jesus *was* God. He was the ladder stretching from heaven to earth, connecting the holy with the human. By eating with sinners, Jesus put His love of people over piety. But those who worry about good manners don't understand this. Which is why the religious resisted with such vehemence.

Back in the 1950s and '60s, a researcher by the name of Harry Harlow did a number of studies on attachment by observing rhesus monkeys. These studies took place before the advent of animal protection guidelines, and I should warn you his methods would not fly today. But Harlow's results were stunning and significant. And I couldn't pull myself away from the grainy black-and-white videos documenting his research.

To begin, Harlow separated baby monkeys from their mothers a few hours after birth. Then he made two surrogate "mothers," the first out of hard, cold wire with a milk bottle mounted on the top, and the second covered in soft terry cloth but without the bottle. Then the baby monkeys were given a choice of mothers and Harlow recorded their responses. Although the monkeys went to the wire mother for food, they spent the majority of their time cuddled with the terry-cloth mother, even though she offered no physical sustenance.

Harlow theorized that attachment was not about food and water, hunger and thirst. It was about relationship. Over and over, the monkeys preferred a soft, nurturing "mother" over food, even when they were hungry. Because they ached for more than milk; they ached for love, safety, touch, and connection.[49]

The church—and the people who make up the church—don't always do a good job of providing a soft place for hungry people. Instead, we draw lines and serve our food to those we deem deserve it. We're far more concerned with hard-wire boundaries than terry-cloth comfort.

While it is true we need rules, boundaries, and responsibilities to guide families and society, we need more than functional, cold-wire apparatuses to deliver what we crave. We need food in the context of relationship.

Which is what went down at the Last Supper table.

The table Jesus shared with His closest friends included common laborers, tax collectors, uneducated fishermen, a guy with an anger problem, and another with a doubt problem. Several at His table boasted egos bigger than their pay grade, and one was secretly selling his proximity to Jesus for a kickback he would later regret.

These were not the rule-following, line-drawing pious. These were ordinary, everyday broken people who were likely to launch ground beef onto the shoulder of their tablemate while saying something decidedly unreligious.

Even so. Jesus offered each a seat at His table. Bread spread out before them, His body close enough to squeeze a shoulder, slap a back, or touch a hand. He invited them to dinner, said, "Do life with Me. You are family. I love you." And in the process, He fed more than their bellies.

It wasn't about the food. It was about relationship.

"While they were eating, Jesus took bread, and when he had given thanks, he broke it and gave it to his disciples, saying, 'Take it; this is my body'" (Mark 14:22).

One by one, they took the bread, tore some off, chewed, swallowed, and passed it on.

"Then he took a cup, and when he had given thanks, he gave it to them, and they all drank from it" (v. 23).

They *all* drank from it, egomaniacs and doubters and deniers alike.

"This is my blood of the covenant" (v. 24).

The covenant. The covenant cut with Abraham. The covenant promising God would bless not only one man but every last one of us. The animals, cut in bloody pieces, separated to form a path that God alone would walk through. If the relationship was broken, the attachment breached, He would be the one torn in two to make everything—everyone—whole.

"This is my blood of the covenant, which is poured out for many" (v. 24).

He came and sat at our table so the many would never again fear losing their seats at His.

It wasn't about consuming but about pouring. It was never about the meal. It was always about the relationship. An invitation to a covenantal, table-sharing intimacy. And the price He was willing to pay to secure it.

Poured out for many. The great and the small, the whole and the broken, the strong and the weak, the sick and the well. No longer would there be any boundaries, any separation, any breach, any divide.

Only one table. One cup. One meal. And terry-cloth grace.

⸙

I met Susan about fifteen years ago when she joined the Bible study I led at our home church. We both had three grade-school children and a deep love for Jesus which made us fast and furious friends. Then one day she sat next to me at Bible study and told me she was pregnant with her fourth child.

"On purpose?!" I asked.

Not helpful, I realize that now. But I couldn't comprehend that someone would willingly have twice the number of children as adults in their family. Who does that? We all know how that goes down in restaurants.

A few months later, her daughter Kariss was born, a precious blond-haired beauty. Her name was no accident; *charis* is Greek for "grace." Susan saw grace in what life delivered. Having overcome a hard childhood, she found Jesus in adulthood, much like my Dad. While I'd launch into panic at the thought of more children, Susan welcomed it. Which is what happened once again when, three years later, Kariss welcomed a little brother named Jackson. Yep, Susan added number five to the mix. The offspring tally was now Michele 3, Susan 5.

Clearly, I was winning.

Susan and I didn't see each other much during the following years. Who had the time? When we did manage to get together, it looked a bit like a traveling county fair. Kids, sticky fingers, and chaos everywhere. Every now and then, I'd remind her—smug and self-satisfied—that we'd be empty nesters sitting on a beach savoring retirement while they still parented their two final kids at home. We thought we were quite hilarious.

But the laughter dimmed in 2010, when I was diagnosed with cancer for the first time. A couple of months later, the four of us gathered once again—Troy and me, Susan and her husband, Ric. We went out for dinner and an NBA basketball game. And over fish tacos and free throws, we processed what it was like to be thirty-nine with a cancer diagnosis. I was terrified. But Susan showed nothing but her characteristic grace and peace. It was as if she wanted to will me to believe: *It's going to be okay, Michele. It's all going to be okay.*

It was a year or more before we saw each other again. We gathered for Easter brunch. But this time, the Cushatts had added three extra bunnies to the table, all younger than Jackson. Of course, that put the parenting score at Susan 5, Michele 6.

I was no longer winning.

Susan and Ric would be lounging on the beach while Troy and I would likely transition straight from parenting to the nursing home. I did not find God's humor amusing.

But while the rest of us laughed at the fact of eleven children between our two households, Susan saw it all as a gift. She welcomed the chaos, the additional chairs around the table. To her, it was evidence of God's beautiful grace.

I never expected to see her May 12, 2015. That day was my post-treatment PET scan. The day when doctors took a hard look at my insides to see whether the chemo and radiation they'd been throwing at me had actually done their job.

PET scan days are hard days. They shake me up like a can of soda, reminding me of my mortality and how everything can explode in a moment. After I finished my scan, I wanted to make a beeline to my car and go home. I grabbed my purse and jacket and headed out to the waiting room to make my escape on the other side.

That's when I saw Susan and Ric. This time we did not share a meal or laughter. Instead, Susan shared the news that she'd just been diagnosed with breast cancer.

It was the day after her diagnosis, those early pregnant hours when no one has any answers and everyone is scrambling to make sense and plans. She was there for her own PET scan.

We huddled together, talking in hushed tones, Susan and Ric sharing what they knew and what they still waited to find out. And then, when we had no more words, we prayed. The three of us wrapped our arms around each other right there in our waiting room chairs and asked God to show us His glory.

Himself.

I still marvel at the timing of that day, how out of so many possible doctors, offices, and appointment times, our PET scans ended up shoulder to shoulder with each other. I knew it then as much as I know it now: our shared moment around that table of circumstance was no accident.

A few weeks later, Susan and I met for breakfast at one of our favorite restaurants. By then, she was neck deep in chemotherapy. Her hair was gone, and in its place was a wig she didn't want to wear.

"My kids think I should wear it. But it makes me itch." We laughed, as best we could.

Neither of us could eat much. I still hadn't made much progress using my new mouth. And chemo blisters covered the inside of Susan's. Even so, as we boxed up our leftover pancakes to take home and feed to our families, we both felt full. Our breakfast date wasn't about the food. It was about how much we needed each other in this hard place.

In the months following, we both carried burdens neither of us wished for or wanted. And rarely were we well enough to share the same room or the same table. And yet we held vigil with each other in prayers and text messages when we could.

Thirteen months later, Susan was back in the hospital. By then I had recovered enough to resume traveling and speaking, a modicum of my previous life. Susan, however, had relapsed. After ten months of treatments and surgeries, she had been declared cancer free. But a short eight weeks later, cancer was back with a vengeance.

I spent her last weekend in the hospital with her and her family. Talking about her favorite worship songs, reading her favorite Bible verses. Sunday, midmorning, right as the rest of the world went out for brunch, my dear friend Susan breathed her last.

To her final exhalation, she did not waver. She knew her God. She believed Him and trusted Him. Even when she couldn't have evidence of Him in a miraculous healing.

Charis. Grace.

She already had what she'd been looking for.

It's now been two years since Susan left us. And last week we gathered at the family's home to remember the anniversary of her death. Her children greeted guests, and Ric grilled enough hot dogs, hamburgers, and brats for an army. And that army brought enough side dishes to feed themselves and the rest of the neighborhood.

There was no agenda or structure. We all came when we could, sat around crowded tables and kitchen islands and talked about life.

Susan would have liked it, I think. Because we didn't make it all about her. And we certainly didn't make it about death.

Our meal together was about life, the life each one of us has yet to live. As we slurped watermelon slices and stuffed our faces with bratwurst, we were gently reminded, once again, that life is precious. Fragile. Easily lost.

But at the same time, we remembered that in all its fragility, life is also a beautiful gain. It is an offering of food that is best savored by pulling up chairs around a shared table. Some of us limp there, broken and beat up. Some of us, filled with an extra measure of grace, share our portion with those hungry for a little extra.

The wine and the cup. The body and the blood. Shared and swallowed by all of us.

I drove home, missing my friend with a fresh ache. But I felt a measure of peace knowing she doesn't miss what she left behind. She now sits at a different table, a bigger and more lasting table filled with everything she once longed for but could never find.

Her short forty-seven years of life were merely the appetizer, the warmup.

And I like to think that, maybe, she's pulled a chair up next to my dad's and they're both stuffing themselves like gluttons on grace.

"I am the way and the truth and the life," He said (John 14:6).

Death, yes. But more important, life.

⋄

It is Sunday, and I sit with my family eight rows from the communion table.

The blood of the covenant. The sacrifice cut in two, the lamb slain to satisfy the hunger.

One man broken so all of mankind could be made whole.

For me, taking communion is difficult. I have to chew the wafer, slowly, trying to turn the tiny pieces in my mouth with a tongue that no longer works and wash them down with a cup of juice that's far too small. I'm tempted to skip communion altogether, pass the tray to the stranger to my left.

But I catch myself before the bitter taste of struggle steals the sweetness of the sacrament.

Jesus has pulled out a chair for me.

Have you found what you've been looking for? He asks, reaching for me.

He urges me to come, to take my place at His table, just as I am.

Charis. Grace.

I look at the scars carving up my arm, feel the mouth that no longer works, consider the wounds passed from generation to generation, down to my father and finally to me and my children. It's hard to take a seat at this table and let myself be seen exactly as I am.

And then I remember I'm not the only one with scars.

I close my eyes, picture His face, His hands, His side, His feet. And I take my seat. The one He's been waiting for me to receive. If He could sit broken at my table, I can sit broken at His.

It isn't about the food. It's about the relationship. The relentless presence that finally satisfies the hunger nothing else could ever fill.

And I offer my broken body right back to Him.

ALTAR STONE 10

LOOKING FOR GOD'S PRESENCE IN YOUR HUNGER

I don't do well tolerating difficult emotions. Whether it is pain, rejection, loneliness, or longing, I want a quick fix, something to numb my discomfort and make the pain go away. At times, this has led me to be impulsive and reactive or to toy with addictions that invariably disappoint. But part of maturing and healing is learning to tolerate difficult emotions, to see them not as problems to be solved but as emotions to be honored. To sit with my loneliness or soul hunger is not to ignore it but to acknowledge what it says about the one who made me. What is your ongoing hunger? What human need continually rises up to cause you discomfort? There is evidence of God's presence there. Pray for God to open your eyes to see what you have missed. Then write it down. Mark it. This is your tenth altar stone.

I've spent considerable hours contemplating my parents' upbringing and bondage issues and have gained great empathy for them both. They were products of the Great Depression. My dad served in the CCCs in the Grand Canyon building the trails when he was very young, and it had a huge negative impact on him. They both grew up in different but harsh homes. They both struggled with alcoholism during a cultural time period where families didn't know how to address dysfunction. They had tragically lost a child. They had experienced divorce during a time when that was taboo. I'm not making excuses for their sinfulness or for their wrong choices—I have gained an understanding and that has helped set me free.

For that I am eternally grateful.

—DAD, DECEMBER 8, 2011

CHAPTER 11

A Cross

A GOD WHO IS WITH YOU IN PAIN, SUFFERING, AND DEATH

For those willing to stay awake, pain remains a reliable altar in the world, a place to discover that a life can be as full of meaning as it is of hurt. The two have never canceled each other out and I doubt they ever will, at least not until each of us—or all of us together—find a way through.

—BARBARA BROWN TAYLOR, *AN ALTAR IN THE WORLD*

It is through death that we deeply touch life.

—HENRI NOUWEN

I walked through the sea of ancient gravestones in silence.

An ocean and a nine-hour plane ride separated me from my family. Hundreds of years and several generations separated me from my ancestors. And yet as I stood in the soft grass warmed by the Cornish sun on my face, I felt the past and the present merging into one pregnant moment.

My trip to the United Kingdom had come in response to a speaking invitation. More than five hundred Jesus-loving women of various denominations and backgrounds gathered in Plymouth for their annual women's conference. They'd asked me to be one of their keynote speakers, to share my hard story of faith in places of suffering. It remains one of my most treasured events. It is only now—more than a year and a half later—that I see the fingerprints of God's presence and provision on the invitation.

I'd long wanted to travel to the United Kingdom. My father's name—and my maiden name—is Trethewey, an English name meaning "Land of David" and common to Cornwall, the county at the southwesternmost tip of England. For much of my childhood, Dad regaled us with tales of our Cornish heritage, including of a great-great-great-grandfather who sailed from Cornwall in the mid-1850s to try his hand at mining in America. Although I grew up far removed from both Cornwall and mining, evidence of our Cornish heritage remained in the tea with cream my grandparents drank, the many months my dad spent in Arizona's copper mines in college, and the meat and potatoes "pasties" my mom made for dinner.

Although Dad always dreamed of traveling back to his ancestors' homeland, he never made it. So when I realized my speaking engagement would take me to within a short train ride of Cornwall, I tacked a few more days onto my trip. This was my chance to connect some of the dots of our family's story. Then when an online friend living in Cornwall, Sherry, reached out and offered to be my tour guide, all the pieces fell into place.

For five days Sherry and her husband, Patrick, guided my mom and me through more Cornish landscape and history than I would've been able to cover on my own, including ancient fishing harbors, abandoned copper mines, and an ancient Anglican church in St. Stephen-in-Brannel, a small Cornwall parish a short drive from where we stayed in Penzance. We visited other parishes before this one, walked through old churches and cemeteries. But when I walked through the iron gate of St. Stephen to the tombstone-riddled courtyard within, I noticed this one felt almost familiar, like home.

Dedicated August 20, 1261, the St. Stephen Parish Church

stands like a regal queen in the center of the community. With its imposing four-spired tower, multiple stained-glass windows, and gray stones, the church took me back in time. Grave markers from hundreds of years before showed the effects of weather and age, many covered with moss and leaning to one side or the other, much of the text difficult to read. I walked down the path, occasionally veering off to scour names and dates for any I recognized.

With the four of us searching and the noon bells of St. Stephen keeping us company, we covered nearly every inch of the churchyard and adjoining cemetery. In all, we found at least a dozen markers with the name Trethewey. I touched each one with respect, knowing it was possible that beneath the earth at my feet lay the remains of someone who once shared my DNA.

It wasn't until the end, when the groundskeeper offered to help us scan old death records, that I was informed of the near impossibility of such. As it turns out, Trethewey is as common a Cornish name as Smith or Jones is an American one. Even so, I left St. Stephen only mildly disappointed. After buying a large box of Cornish tea from the store across the street, I drove away still believing I'd walked on sacred familial ground, regardless of the groundskeeper's doubt.

It took more than a year to finally discover I was right.

Before Dad passed, a cousin sent him a collection of genealogy records she'd compiled of their family line, dating from the early thirteenth century. A few weeks ago, Mom found them on Dad's old laptop. And when she did, she forwarded them to me. Close to fifty typed pages of history I'd never seen. And buried in the middle of it, I found gold: "The fifth child of John III and Mary Truskett Trethewey, James E., was christened on June 30, 1816, in St. Stephen, Cornwall, England. He married a Jane Wallace (Wallish) on October 17, 1840, in St. Stephen, Cornwall, England. James and his family immigrated to Canada in about 1850, settling at Bowmanville/Fort Hope area on Lake Ontario. They had five sons and two daughters."

James E. Trethewey. My great-great-great-grandfather. The one who brought our family to North America. He was baptized and married in St. Stephen Church. His parents and his parents' parents as well. And in the midst of all my churchyard wandering that May day in St. Stephen-in-Brannel, his story and mine had, in fact, intersected. And the God of us both brought from death a glimmer of new life.

⁂

The document is dated December 8, 2011. But I didn't find it until I was halfway done writing this book.

I remember dialing Dad's number on a late afternoon, a vague sense of urgency driving me. When he answered, I asked him to write his story, telling him that if he didn't put words on paper, his story would be lost to all of us when he was gone.

Of course, I had no way of knowing when I said those words how truly urgent they were. He was still a healthy, active, sixty-seven-year-old man, enjoying his wife, children, and grandchildren and the first years of his retirement. None of us knew that eighteen months later he would be diagnosed with pancreatic cancer, and that thirteen months after that he would be gone.

The document came to me a few months ago, when random circumstance shook loose the memory of that phone call. After scouring my digital files and coming up empty, I shot my mom a text to ask her if she knew about it. She didn't but promised to search his old laptop computer.

She texted me less than an hour later.

"I think I found it. Check your email."

The moment I clicked it open, I knew.

"I am writing this legacy of my personal family memories at the request of my Princess. She said to me, 'Dad, if you don't write it, it will be lost forever.' Well, maybe this quote isn't quite word for word, but it is close. It deeply touched my heart, so I have decided to honor her request."

I could hear his voice as I read his words, as if he reached across the breach between us to take care of this last piece of unfinished business. And although I couldn't articulate why, I knew I needed it. I needed to see his words and hear his story. Somehow his story was tangled up in mine, and I suspected I wouldn't find the healing I longed for until I was able to unravel the two.

Even so, I couldn't make it past the first paragraph that day. It took two months to find the courage to read all of Dad's words. There were still too many knots, too many unresolved questions and untended wounds. My hunger for truth was at war with my need to self-protect. I'd been bleeding for too long, and I wasn't sure I could endure another letting. So once again, I pushed him away, afraid of getting too close, of entering into the pain—his and mine.

Then a day came when I knew it was time.

While my children played in the front yard, the sounds of their carefree voices filtering through my open window, I sat down at my laptop, found the document I was looking for, and pressed Print.

Fourteen pages, single spaced. The final words of my father's life. He began with a disclaimer: "I have no intent to defame anyone. Nor do I wish to relate only the negative experiences in my life. I wish to capture the fullness of my life—both those which may seem to be either negative or positive, some I'm proud of and some I'm ashamed of—but all reflect my growing up years and have helped to shape the person I am.

"My life is my life," he admitted. "But naturally only as I saw it. Some might be just my perception of the event/experience. At the same time, I sincerely believe most of what I share is what really occurred, or I wouldn't share it."

I shook my head at the irony. I'd penned a similar disclaimer in the early pages of this book. He understood that no matter our diligence in piecing fragments of memory into an accurate history, we cannot escape bias and the way our perceptions shape what we grow to believe. Whether he intended them to or not, his words offered permission, giving me the freedom to name my experience and, perhaps, one day find healing through it.

I didn't make it past page two before the first crack appeared in my emotional dam. By page three, I was drowning. With every word, one more chunk of cement broke loose. What he'd recorded in those fourteen pages was a summary of the intimate, defining traumas that marked him during his early years. And thus marked me. I've included excerpts of the less horrific experiences in between each chapter in this book. Although he'd hinted at these stories while he was alive, I wasn't yet ready to hear them.

Now, as I read each page, I didn't see a sixty-seven-year-old man making excuses for his anger.

I saw an eleven-year-old boy finally telling someone the truth about his pain.

I saw my father. And I saw my children. Innocent eleven-year-olds who suffered too many abuses, separated by two generations.

Dad suffered in the 1940s and '50s, when the world attempted to recover from an economic depression and two world wars. No one then really understood the impact of trauma and PTSD. Harlow's monkeys, Bowlby's theory of attachment, and the ACE study had yet to offer insight.

My children suffered in the subsequent century, when science had already proved the impacts of early childhood trauma and the necessity of safe relationships. Even so, before they were old enough to enter kindergarten, they found themselves at the mercy of broken grownups who couldn't overcome addiction long enough to offer any kind of real love.

Separated by nearly seventy years, these children both craved connection and feared it. They daily fought a war between a biological need to connect and a painful reality that made them terrified of doing so. They both reached and raged, sometimes multiple times in the same day.

And then I saw myself, sandwiched between them. A daughter to one and a mother to the others.

The little girl who spent so much of her life chasing after a father who knew how to be a dictator but didn't always know how to be a daddy.

And the grown woman who, even still, struggles to push through her pain and trauma to connect with the children who can't navigate their own.

I've shared a home with these wounded souls during the two separate halves of my life. It hasn't been easy. Dad did his best to heal, I know. "I selected psychology as my college major in order to better understand myself," he said in his final letter. Dad wanted to heal and, in the process of understanding himself, become a different man, a different father. A man who didn't pass more pain on to yet another generation.

I want to heal too. My long hours in a counselor's office and the thousands of words I've written documenting my struggle prove my determination to do better, to live whole. Even so, recent conversations with my children reveal I've passed on wounds I never intended to.

Sometimes no matter how hard you work to push back the darkness, pain still finds a way to sneak back in. And sometimes healing takes more than one degree, one counselor, or one generation. And more grace and grit than ordinary humans can muster.

Until I faced my own mortality, I didn't appreciate the crucifixion. Now, like a moth to the light, I'm drawn by the story's drama and significance. But it's not so much the radiance of the resurrection that captures me, as full of good news as it is.

It's the dark, bloody struggle that precedes it that I can't get over.

The long night in the garden of Gethsemane after the Last Supper. The complexity of individuals' capacity for both good and evil. The betrayal of one close friend and the abandonment of the others. The arrest by religious leaders and the unfair trial. The abuse, torture, and evidence of evil lurking in ordinary, upstanding citizens. And the gruesome events culminating in hours of daylight darkness and the death of God-with-Us.

The pain of Thursday, Friday, and Saturday speaks to me far more deeply than the joy that comes on Sunday. Although I'm relieved at the resurrection, I'm deeply comforted by the crucifixion. I don't know that I could accept the nearness of a God who knows nothing of my pain. Without some measure of empathy, there is no real connection. God might seem powerful, strong, forgiving, and tolerant. But He would not seem loving.

But the cross changes all that.

When my children were younger, they asked us to put sticky, glow-in-the-dark stars on the ceiling of their bedrooms so that at night when we turned off the lights, their bedrooms would light up with homemade constellations, a childlike simulation of a magnificent night sky.

It was cheap and cheesy, and we had tried to talk them out of the hassle of it. But they loved it, like only those who haven't outgrown their imagination can.

As lovely as those plastic stars were to a child, they couldn't compare to the star-riddled sky spread like a canopy outside their bedroom windows. No number of plastic stars could help them comprehend the vastness of the real thing—a true night sky filled with stars and galaxies, suns and moons, planets and constellations. No matter how many stickers lit up their ceiling, they couldn't wrap their little minds around the power and potency of a single flaming star.

Lately I've been thinking how we've turned the cross into tiny plastic stars. In our efforts to make it something we can hold in our hands, we've lost something of the magnitude and horror of it. We rush to the resolution but miss the narrative agony leading up to it in the thousands of years before. Crucifixes and cross necklaces make death less traumatic. They turn the complex into something containable and easier to comprehend.

But the cost of oversimplification is that we utterly miss how God's trauma intersects with our own.

Pain is plentiful before the abundance of the promised land. Wilderness wandering, sacrifice making, question asking, and far more crosses than resurrections. Jesus stepped neck deep into the messy middle of humanity's raging Jordan River. And He started talking about the kingdom of God as if it's right here, right now, sitting in the bull's-eye center of everything that's wrong with the world. He spoke comfort and performed miracles that made the low ceilings of our lives light up with magic. And for a time, the world felt good and full of hope.

And then it all turned dark one night in a garden, a garden far removed from the one called Eden, where everything went to hell, trauma ripped open relationships, and humankind first experienced pain, suffering, and separation.

In this garden, the one called Gethsemane, Jesus gathered Peter, James, and John and moved deeper into the darkness. These were the same three who watched as Jesus' clothes turned white as lightning on the mountain. This time, however, Jesus didn't shine with glory. Instead, He was sandwiched between His love for His Father and His love for us, His eyes brimmed with weeping.

"Father, if you are willing, take this cup from me" (Luke 22:42).

Please, God. Please. If there is any way . . .

And yet even as His humanity begged for deliverance, His divine heart swelled with relationship.

"Yet not my will, but yours be done."

We must never forget our human instinct to distance ourselves from the horror of the crucifixion. We want something we can stick on our ceilings and gaze at every now and then. But it's far more vast and dangerous and consuming than we can imagine or dare hope.

The prophet Isaiah put the human ache for relationship to poetry and prophecy:

> In all their affliction he was afflicted,
> and the angel of his presence saved them;
> in his love and in his pity he redeemed them;
> he lifted them up and carried them all the days of old.
>
> —ISAIAH 63:9 ESV

I read these words a few weeks ago, although not for the first time. But this time I stumbled on the word "presence."

His presence saved them. What did that mean?

After some searching, I discovered the Hebrew word for "presence" here is *paneh,* which comes from the root "to turn."[50] It can mean face or front, as in a person turning to face you. It's common for the face of a person to be associated with their presence with you. In Jesus, God turned His face toward us, not away.

And in a beautiful poetic irony, the word for "carried" is the Hebrew *nasa,*[51] which means "to raise, lift up" (as in the face, the eyes, the voice, or the soul). It also means "to bear or carry."

Although I am no theologian, do you see hints of what Isaiah is prophesying and God is accomplishing?

In the depths of our worst affliction and suffering, the pain and crises and heartaches that crush us under their weight, God does not turn away. Instead, He yokes Himself with our affliction, carrying it right along with us. He turns His face toward us. And in the process, He lifts our heavy heads so we know we're seen, known, carried, and loved.

When I close my eyes, I can almost picture it, the tender hand of God lifting my chin and face streaked with pain so I don't miss the truth that He is near, His face to mine, even in my darkness. What kind of god would ever stoop so low?

As Brennan Manning writes, "I could more easily contain Niagara Falls in a tea cup than I can comprehend the wild, uncontainable love of God."[52]

Beginning somewhere around the ninth century, the Western Christian church, beginning with the Roman Catholic Church, celebrated those three days preceding Easter with a different kind of service. A Latin word that literally means "darkness," *tenebrae* is experienced on three consecutive days—Maundy Thursday, Good Friday, and Holy Saturday, that long silent day in between death and resurrection.

Each tenebrae service builds on the one the day before, in a darkened room lit only by a handful of candles. Each day, the candles are extinguished one by one until only one is left: the Christ candle.

Participants are encouraged to focus on the pain, the loss, the grief God endured in the garden of Gethsemane, the rejections of Peter and His disciples, the injustice of His arrest and trial, the accusations and beatings of His oppressors, and finally the physical agony of His horrific crucifixion and death.

At that final service, after a Friday that feels anything but good, the final candle is extinguished, the Christ candle blown out while echoing Jesus' words two thousand years old: "It is finished." Then, silent, churchgoers exit tenebrae and leave the community of their congregation in darkness, left to contemplate the blackness of a world without the light of the living grace of God.

Henri Nouwen writes, "Life is a school in which we are trained to depart. That is what mortification really means: training to die, to cut away the enslaving ties with the past. So that what we call death is not a surprise anymore, but the last of many gateways that lead to the full human person."[53]

I've never experienced a tenebrae service, but I've known a deep and consecutive darkness of soul in which every light is extinguished and every hope-full voice silenced. In those moments, walled in by suffering, it seems as if the entire world has gone mad, not least of all myself. There is no hope, no silver lining, no future to look forward to. I'm weighted to the ground in the perpetuity of my grief. No glory, only tears.

This is why some parishioners savor tenebrae. And this is why I savor the days before Sunday. Because Jesus, too, knows that kind of darkness. Jesus, too, felt the ache of separation that His circumstances created. He knows the pain of feeling abandoned by those He loves. Jesus, too, knows what it is like to beg His Father for deliverance from pain but to have to walk through it and feel it anyway.

The difference? Jesus chose suffering. I didn't.

Jesus could've run away, hidden Himself from those who would hurt Him. He knew what awaited Him and He could've put a plan in place to escape it. Only He didn't. He marched "face like flint" toward it (Isa. 50:7). He may have prayed for relief while weeping in the garden, but when the moment of decision came, He chose to enter in. I'm pretty confident I would not do the same.

> He was oppressed and afflicted,
> yet he did not open his mouth;
> he was led like a lamb to the slaughter,
> and as a sheep before its shearers is silent,
> so he did not open his mouth.
>
> —ISAIAH 53:7

He took the verbal abuse, the mockery and face slaps, the ripped scalp and lacerated back. He absorbed the physical torture and emotional trauma. And although it crushed His body, it didn't crush His heart.

Until God turned away, and He was left to endure it alone.

"My God!" He cried out, calling the God He knew as well as Himself.

"Why?!" He asked, knowing the answer but unable to bear it.

"Eli, Eli, lema sabachthani?" (Matt. 27:46).

My God, My God, why have You forsaken Me?

In a deluge of horrific blows, this is the only one that devastated Him. When God removed His presence, turned His *paneh* away and left Him to die.

This is our greatest fear, that when the worst comes to pass, we will find ourselves alone. That the God we've always loved will turn His face or vanish like smoke, proving to be either a mirage and an illusion or an indifferent and absent father.

Why have You forsaken me?

This is what Dad feared in the deep dark of his childhood. And this is what my children fear every time ordinary life reminds them of a time when those who claimed to love them turned their backs on their pain.

And this is what I feared in the dark basement of my own cross, when the will to live was swallowed whole by the pain of living.

But on the cross, the wound we most fear became Jesus'. After spending eternity in relationship with God and the Holy Spirit, Jesus was cut off from communion with the Trinity. Pushed outside the circle of relationship.

Alone.

It was the same kind of separation that Adam and Eve walked through when they exited the garden. The same kind of aching separation you and I experience when a parent fails us, a first love leaves us, a child rejects us. It's the pain we feel when our churches and families split, close friendships splinter, and leaders falter. It's a ripping, a tearing of tender emotional flesh that leaves us bleeding and reeling, strung up on the crosses of our brokenness.

Eli, Eli, lema sabachthani?

Having done nothing wrong, having given His love and His life for His Father and His friends, Jesus experienced one final and fatal injustice—God turned His face away.

"When the sun had set and darkness had fallen, a smoking firepot with a blazing torch appeared and passed between the pieces. On that day the Lord made a covenant" (Gen. 15:17–18).

With the turn of God's face, Jesus carried the cost of our broken covenant. Knowing the price would kill us, Jesus suffered our agony, enduring aloneness so we would never have to.

Positioned between two criminals hanging on the crosses they deserved, Jesus reached His arms out to both. Like a ladder reaching between heaven and earth. And as the day turned dark, God alone walked through the pieces.

"It is finished" (John 19:30).

A promise kept. A relationship healed. A child home. This is the moment to which every other story and verse points. With those three words, Jesus accomplished what every genealogy and family tree aches for.

We think redemption was the goal. But death and resurrection were the necessary means to accomplishing God's relentless desire all along.

To be *with us*.

> Who shall separate us from the love of Christ? Shall trouble or hardship or persecution or famine or nakedness or danger or sword? As it is written:
>
> > "For your sake we face death all day long;
> > we are considered as sheep to be slaughtered."
>
> No, in all these things we are more than conquerors through him who loved us. For I am convinced that neither death nor life, neither angels nor demons, neither the present nor the future,

> nor any powers, neither height nor depth, nor anything else in all creation, will be able to separate us from the love of God that is in Christ Jesus our Lord.
>
> —ROMANS 8:35–39

Weeks before Dad died, we waited for word from his doctor about whether the chemotherapy had worked. For months I'd prayed audacious, believing prayers, knowing that the Jesus who healed the sick and raised the dead could easily say the word and send cancer packing.

But when Dad called one evening with the doctor's report, I heard the hitch in his voice.

"There's nothing more they can do, Michele. We've done all we could. It's over."

My heart sank. I hung up the phone, indignant.

God, why?! I don't understand. I prayed for good *news!*

And although I received no audible reply, I heard my crucified Jesus just the same.

You do have the Good News, Michele. Every last one of you.

It is finished.

In a family tree riddled with so much distance, pain, and dysfunction, we still ended up a family of four found by Jesus. Every last one of us. Dad, in spite of his good intentions, didn't do it all right. Neither did I. Instead, his wound became my wound, and we both ended up broken.

But on the cross? My wound—and Dad's wound—became Jesus' wound.

And we both ended up whole.

ALTAR STONE 11

LOOKING FOR GOD'S PRESENCE IN PAIN AND DEATH

The most difficult place to find evidence of God's presence is in pain. The more we hurt, the more we feel alone. And the more we feel alone, the more convinced we become that God is absent or indifferent. And yet I believe with all my heart that God is where the pain is. Always. Like a moth to light, God draws near to those who weep, mourn, struggle, fail, and long for someone to save them. "The Lord is close to the brokenhearted and saves those who are crushed in spirit," Psalm 34:18 says. Do you see evidence of God in the places of your pain? Have you seen a glimpse of His glory even in the darkness of death? Pray for God to open your eyes to see what you have missed. Then write it down. Mark it. This is your eleventh altar stone.

I started reading. I poured myself into reading the Bible, reading self-help books, marriage and parenting books, and leadership books. I knew how I didn't want to be a husband, parent, friend, leader. I knew I had to learn how to be a healthy one of each of these. I felt God's transforming power in me. He was softening me, He was shaping me, and He was guiding me to understand that He had a plan for using my past for His glory and for His kingdom work.

—DAD, DECEMBER 8, 2011

CHAPTER 12

AN INDWELLING

A GOD WHOSE PRESENCE LIVES IN YOU

O Holy Spirit, descend plentifully into my heart. Enlighten the dark corners of this neglected dwelling and scatter there Thy cheerful beams.

—AUGUSTINE OF HIPPO

Though he tarry, wait for him, for he that shall come will come, though not in our time.

—MATTHEW HENRY, *MATTHEW HENRY'S COMMENTARY ON THE WHOLE BIBLE*

I was seven years old when I took my first piano lesson.

Tuesday evenings, after we rode the bus home from school, my mom loaded us up in our 1980s Ford Granada (if you're not old enough to know that fine piece of automotive genius—may it rest in peace—we cannot be friends) and drove us even deeper into the Midwestern corn and bean fields we called home. Waiting for us at the end of our drive sat a classic white-sided farmhouse, a farmer, and his piano-teacher wife, Mrs. Bowen.

I spent thirty minutes with Mrs. Bowen every week for ten solid years. She greeted us in a dress most days, always had something savory cooking in the kitchen, and wore a crown of perfectly rolled salt-and-pepper hair that I take partial credit for (the color, not the rolls).

I was a child who couldn't tolerate mistakes. Unfortunately, learning to play the piano comes with a fair amount of mistakes. This made me at times—how should I say?—insufferable. Even for a seven-year-old. I wanted to go from novice to concert pianist without the years of painstaking practice in between.

At the time, Mrs. Bowen appeared ancient to my grade-school eyes. She likely was in her fifties when I first sat down on her piano bench. Shockingly close to my age right now, Jesus help me. I don't recall a single time she criticized or barked a rebuke, although there were times I deserved it.

I have many fond memories of my time with Mrs. Bowen. Not included in that collection, though, were her twice-a-year recitals.

Performing terrified me. Not because I couldn't play the piano. Truth is I learned the theory and technique quickly and executed both well. My terror was nothing more than a fear of public failure. I couldn't bear the thought of making a mistake in front of so many familiar faces.

Of the more than twenty recitals in which I performed, one stands out from the others. I can still picture the room, the piano, and what happened when it was my turn to play.

My piece was called "Cripple Creek." I still have it in a box in the basement, one floor below where I now sit. I'd practiced it for weeks, memorized every note, could play it in my sleep. Not only had I mastered "Cripple Creek," I loved playing it. This was the first piece that made me feel like a pianist, requiring both the skill and speed of experience.

I was ready.

Until I climbed onto that stage and stole a peek at the packed room. Then I panicked. My throat closed, my skin turned clammy, my heart started pounding like that of a cornered animal. Having nowhere to go, I lowered myself onto the piano bench, tucked my skirt underneath, then lifted my hands to the keys.

My shaking, trembling hands.

How would I do this? The piece was too fast, too tricky. And my fingers were no longer under my control.

The silence weighed heavily; everyone was waiting. I had no choice but to begin.

I made it through the first measures and lines, my fingers working from muscle memory. But the more I played, the more my fingers approached a speed they couldn't maintain. Faster and faster until they hit a velocity that made them stumble all over each other.

At the first mistake, I froze. I could no longer remember the music I'd worked so hard to memorize, had zero idea of my next note. Suddenly, the room that had been filled with music turned silent.

I never recovered that day. After more attempts to regain my composure, I stumbled through to the end and nearly ran to my seat, humiliated. My failure haunted me for years, mushrooming my fear of platforms and public mistakes.

Now, looking back, I know better. That seven-year-old girl thought playing the piano was all about the theory, practice, and performance. She believed making a mistake was the worst thing that could happen.

She didn't realize that the bigger mistake is failing to fall in love with the music.

A friend recently told me of a hospitalized man on the edge of death. He spent many days bedridden, fighting for life. One day, in between visits from family and friends, the man felt a presence in his hospital room, hovering at the foot of the bed. Whereas before he'd been wracked with fear and pain, now he felt warm and calm. No pain; overwhelming peace.

But soon the comforting presence turned unbearable. Although I can hardly imagine, he claimed the goodness and glory became too much, and he feared he might die from the intensity of it. It was as if God Himself sat at the foot of his bed. Finally, he cried out, "No more! Don't come any closer, I can't take any more!"

I listened to the story intrigued but skeptical. This wasn't the first time I'd heard friends speak of mysterious experiences of God's presence.

I'm still waiting for mine, however. In spite of many prayers and pleas for God to "show me your glory!" (Ex. 33:18), I've yet to see strange lights, apparitions, or angels, nor have I heard a deep James Earl Jones voice offering divine guidance from the heights of my bedroom ceiling.

A girl can still hope.

Instead, my spiritual life could be best described as long stretches of silence and confusion peppered with brief but rare moments of spiritual clarity that last about as long as a sneeze. I try to hang on to those glory moments, certain that if I could have but a few more seconds of holy nearness it would finally ease my aching. Like grasping air with the hand, it disappears as soon as I reach for it.

But is my lack of awareness indicative of an absence of His presence? I don't think so.

I believe salvation to be one hundred percent God's work, a result of His grace alone (Eph. 2:8–9). There is absolutely nothing I can do to earn it or deserve it. Even my desire for Him is evidence of His grace.

But now I'm starting to understand that spiritual living—the ongoing process of connecting with God and becoming more like Him—is also His work. For too long I assumed all responsibility, working hard to do the do's and avoid the don'ts, to flagellate myself into holiness to prove myself worthy of Him. In a sense, I imitated the Old Testament Israelites, exhausting myself to erect a perfected tabernacle in the hope that God's presence would come down from heaven and be with me.

Here's the problem: when I didn't *feel* God's presence, I assumed the blame. I must've done something wrong, missed some instruction. I both loathed myself for my repeated failures and resented God for His impossible standards. I desperately needed Him but could never measure up to Him.

I'd missed the key message of the new covenant that everything changed with Jesus, when God came down and gave us full access to Himself. That's why the disciples panicked when Jesus said He was going away. What would they do without His nearness?

This is how Jesus responded: "But because I have said these things to you, sorrow has filled your hearts. Nevertheless, I tell you the truth: it is to your advantage that I go away, for if I do not go away, the Counselor will not come to you; but if I go, I will send him to you" (John 16:6–7 RSV).

Jesus' absence was about to make space for an even greater gift: God's presence moving closer still. Not merely dwelling with us but dwelling *in us* (John 14:16–20).

Several months ago, I spent well over an hour on a video consultation with Debi Grebenik, director of the Trauma Training Institute and a well-known expert in trauma therapy and healing for children.[54] Having connected through a mutual friend, I came prepared with a long list of questions and, to be quite honest, frustrations. We were neck deep in the most difficult year of parenting our youngest three children. As they quickly approached adolescence, the memories of their childhood traumas, both conscious and subconscious, turned our household into a war zone. And my own trauma and too-slow emotional and physical healing only added to the intensity. We needed help.

Then came the call with Debi. And in the middle of a few tears and too many questions, she shared a common trauma analogy that shifted my entire mindset.

"Do you know the secret to getting out of a dog bite?" she asked.

What?! I had no idea what she was talking about.

"Let's say you see a dog and reach out your hand to pet it. But rather than welcome your affection, the dog sees you as a threat and attacks. Now your entire fist is trapped between the canine's teeth."

Now that sounded familiar. Living with someone recovering from trauma feels like being caught in a dog's bite. Unpredictable and painful.

"How do you get your hand out with the least amount of damage?" she asked. She didn't wait for an answer.

"Human instinct will make you want to jerk back, yank your hand out of the dog's mouth. But that's when the damage happens." She paused for only a second.

"The secret? Push in."[55]

Push in. It didn't take more than a moment for me to make the connection. And then I burst into tears. When a child or an adult is in the middle of a trauma response, instinct will tell you to pull away, shut down, self-protect. Those who've been deeply wounded often strike out at those around them. But the secret to healing is to push in. To stay close. Then what was once wounded in relationship can be healed in relationship.[56]

This is what Jesus wanted the disciples to understand, what He wants you and me to understand. Although God came close with the covenant, the tabernacle, the incarnation, and the cross, there remained a gap He longed to fill. With the gift of the Holy Spirit, God pushed in until His presence—His living, active presence—took residence *in us*.

I laughed, God help me. The irony was not lost on me. Psychiatrists and trauma professionals thought they'd come up with a brilliant new insight into the healing of humanity's deepest relational wounds.

Turns out, God already had it covered.

⋄

Come with me back to the Jordan River, the place where our journey began.

As you already know, Joshua led God's people across the Jordan, crossing over from their former slavery and wilderness suffering into the promised land. However, in order to move from one to the other, the Israelites had to cross the Jordan River at flood stage, an impossibility.

Thus, God instructed Joshua to have the Levites carrying the ark of the covenant—the container holding God's presence and covered by a mercy seat—stand in the middle of the Jordan. It's important to note that the Levites (those of the tribe of Levi and designated as priests) were the only ones who could come near the ark, and only after extensive washing, rule-following, and preparation. Everyone else had to stay away—the holy power of God's presence would kill anyone who touched it.

But why the Levites? Why not a different tribe? This goes all the way back to Genesis 29, when Jacob's wife Leah kept having babies in the hope that her husband would finally love her.

"Again she conceived, and when she gave birth to a son she said, 'Now at last my husband will become attached to me, because I have borne him three sons.' So he was named Levi" (Gen. 29:34).

Levi, the name of Jacob and Leah's third son and the man who would become the head of God's designated tribe of the priests of God's presence, means "attached."

When these ark-carrying Levites put their feet in the water, the raging Jordan River parted in two, creating an aisle the people could pass through. While the Levites stood holding the ark of the covenant in the center, the people moved from slavery to freedom, from their past to their future.

Now fast-forward thousands of years to a man named John the Baptist. He preached in the wilderness during a period of spiritual wilderness and slavery for God's people. He urged them to repent and turn their hearts back to God. A savior was coming, and they needed to be ready.

Enter Jesus. The incarnation. One day He approaches John the

Baptist while he's baptizing people in the river—the Jordan River. John refuses, knowing to whom he speaks. But Jesus says it has to be done.

And with that, John—a Levite son of his father, Zechariah, a priest—touches Jesus and lowers Him into the water. Immanuel, "God with us," the flesh-and-blood ark of the covenant and container of God's presence and mercy, stands in the middle of the Jordan River. And as John lowers Him, the water doesn't part, but heaven does. The divide between God and man disappears as the Spirit of God descends on Jesus like a ladder connecting heaven to earth.

Three short years later, Jesus dies, stretched out on a cross, crucified between two covenant breakers. As He breathes His last, He walks through the covenantal pieces alone, so we can pass through slavery and suffering to a future full of promise, a new garden of Eden in God's presence.

In the Old Testament, the name Joshua is the Hebrew יְהוֹשֻׁעַ, or *Yehoshu'a,* which means "YAHWEH is salvation." It comes from two root words, *yeho,* which is a reference to the Hebrew God, and *yasha',* which means "to save." Interestingly, the New Testament name Jesus is a Greek variation of Joshua, essentially meaning the same: "The Lord is salvation."

Throughout the Bible, Joshua is seen as a foreshadowing of the true savior who was to come. Just as Joshua succeeded Moses, so the New Testament gospel fulfilled in Jesus succeeded the Old Testament Law. Joshua was anointed after Moses to lead God's people into their "rest," the promised land of Israel. Jesus was *the* anointed one, after all the others, to be the *one* to invite all people into their eternal promised land, rest in relationship with God forerever (Heb. 4:6–11).

When the disciples fled on the night of Jesus' arrest, and then when they watched His brutal death from a distance, everything they'd come to believe the three years before came unhinged. They'd given up their lives to follow Him—family, careers, homes, plans. And what for? To watch Him die?

Like a boat without sails, they gathered behind locked doors in an upstairs meeting room, unmoored and lost. They had zero idea what to do next. Then in the middle of their pain, Jesus entered, passing through walls and locked doors to stand in their midst, close enough to touch.

He was alive! Jesus was alive!

Just that fast, grief turned to joy. Presence does that. For thirty days, during which Jesus continued to teach them, eat with them, comfort them, everything was as it had been before.

Until one day, while He was talking, Jesus was "taken up before their very eyes, and a cloud hid him from their sight" (Acts 1:9). Like a dream disappearing the moment they reached for it.

I hate goodbyes and can imagine the pain of this one. How would they live without Him? How would they know what to do and say without His guiding presence? How would they endure without His encouragement, find strength without His lending it, feel comfort without the sound of His voice offering it?

Then they remembered: "Do not leave Jerusalem, but wait for the gift my Father promised, which you have heard me speak about. For John baptized with water, but in a few days you will be baptized with the Holy Spirit . . . You will receive power when the Holy Spirit comes on you; and you will be my witnesses in Jerusalem, and in all Judea and Samaria, and to the ends of the earth" (1:4–5, 8).

So that's what they did. They waited. And God pushed in.

"When the day of Pentecost came, they were all together in one place. Suddenly a sound like the blowing of a violent wind came from heaven and filled the whole house where they were sitting" (2:1–2).

What happened in the days following Pentecost is recorded in the remaining verses of Acts 2 and a handful of chapters that follow. Quite literally, the disciples were in-spired. The wind of the Holy Spirit filled them, head to toe, and where they felt a void from Jesus' absence, they now experienced an abundant filling of the indwelling presence of God.

For those of us who follow Jesus, this is our gift too. The purpose of the Holy Spirit is to breathe new life into those of us who find ourselves short of breath with the living of it. He is our daily inspiration, giving us even more access to the Father than Jesus did. Like a dying woman hooked up to life support, I'm connected to a constant flow of spiritual oxygen, and with each inhalation of God's presence, I feel the lagging cells of my broken body inspired by God's nearness.

Luke 10:21 gives a vivid picture of what this kind of divine inspiration can accomplish by describing Jesus as "full of joy through the Holy Spirit." The Greek word used for "joy" here means "to leap, skip, dance; to be ecstatic." And again, in Acts 13:52: "And the disciples were filled with joy and with the Holy Spirit." This joy superseded circumstances because it came from within, not without.

Experiencing God's presence isn't about the practice, theory, and performance. It's about falling in love with the music.

It was August 1—the day after my forty-seventh birthday—and I sat right in the middle of Colorado's Red Rocks Amphitheatre.

The tickets had been my birthday present this year. As well as for Mother's Day, our wedding anniversary, Christmas, Valentine's, Halloween. Maybe even Columbus Day. A total of 9,525 seats filled the outdoor theater cut into the red rocks of the Rocky Mountain foothills near Morrison, Colorado. And my husband and I filled two of them.

This was a sold-out concert, complete with heavy traffic and long-distance parking. After climbing what felt like one hundred flights of stairs, we found our seats fifty-five rows up, close to center. Each seat boasted a clear view of the stage and perfect acoustics. Even with more than an hour to go to showtime, the amphitheater pulsed with expectation. Men, women, and children of all ages and nationalities spoke in excited whispers.

As the sun set behind us, a warm orange glow turned the red

rocks of Denver's landmark to fire. Then with every pair of eyes trained on the single chair populating the stage, we waited for the star of the show to make his appearance.

Famed cellist Yo-Yo Ma.

The crowd erupted with enthusiastic applause the moment he walked across the stage, and Yo-Yo Ma smiled and bowed his head in response. Then he sat down, adjusted his chair. And when he raised his bow, the entire place turned silent. Even nature seemed to keep her peace.

Then the first note.

For three hours, I couldn't stop smiling. Yo-Yo Ma performed Bach's *Six Suites for Unaccompanied Cello* to an audience of thousands who savored every note. In between each suite, the crowd stood in a jubilant ovation. The music was life, in all its nuance and complexity, highs and lows, successes and failures. And we inhaled every inspired moment of it.

Mr. Ma executed his performance with precision. Every note, every dynamic. The theory, technique, and interpretation were impeccable, without flaw. But as I listened to him, I didn't marvel at his talent or mastery, although he demonstrated both.

What captivated my attention?

His face.

He smiled. Grinned. Laughed occasionally at some inside joke or private delight. It was as if he played in his living room to a crowd of no one, savoring the sound of each note and the feel of each string. I'm convinced that at times he forgot the fact that ten thousand people watched him.

And it occurred to me—a rusty piano player and communicator who can no longer sing and speak with any kind of precision—that what moved me about Mr. Ma's performance wasn't his talent or execution, although he clearly didn't lack either.

What inspired me was his affection.

Yo-Yo Ma is a man who once upon a time fell in love with music.

And each time he picks up his instrument to play, he remembers and celebrates the romance all over again. He doesn't perform; he inhales the music, and then he exhales it for the rest of us to savor and enjoy. As a result, every last one of us went home inspired and filled to the gills with life.

This is what God accomplishes by giving the Holy Spirit to those of us who dare to wait in our upper rooms as long as it takes for Him to appear. With each note of the symphony composed from Genesis to Revelation, God moved closer to us in a powerful crescendo. In all of life's nuance and complexity, highs and lows, successes and failures, He was there. And for those of us willing to be romanced by His nearness, the narrative of all of creation will lead to a glorious finale.

"Then I saw 'a new heaven and a new earth,' for the first heaven and the first earth had passed away, and there was no longer any sea. I saw the Holy City, the new Jerusalem, coming down out of heaven from God, prepared as a bride beautifully dressed for her husband. And I heard a loud voice from the throne saying, 'Look! God's dwelling place is now among the people, and he will dwell with them. They will be his people, and God himself will be with them and be their God. "He will wipe every tear from their eyes. There will be no more death" or mourning or crying or pain, for the old order of things has passed away'" (Rev. 21:1–4).

In the presence of the one and only, every last one of us will finally be healed. The wounds we've suffered and the wounds we've caused will be made whole by the hand that has been holding us fast in His grip from the day of Eden's fall. And in spite of our years of living in the dark, we will finally see His light.

"I did not see a temple in the city, because the Lord God Almighty and the Lamb are its temple. The city does not need the sun or the moon to shine on it, for the glory of God gives it light, and the Lamb is its lamp" (vv. 22–23).

No longer will we be lonely souls searching for a God who never leaves. Instead, God's home will be with you, with me.

"Fling wide, then, the portals of your soul," Charles Spurgeon writes. "He will come with that love which you long to feel, He will come with that joy into which you cannot work your poor depressed spirit; He will bring the peace which now you have not; He will come with His glass of wine and sweet apples of love, and cheer you till you have no other sickness but that of 'love o'er powering, love divine.' Only open the door to Him, drive out His enemies, give Him the keys of your heart, and he will dwell there forever. Oh, wondrous love, that brings such a guest to dwell in such a heart!"[57]

Come, love that will not let me go. My heart is hungry, the door is open, and the keys are Yours. Always. Woo me with Your relentless nearness, Father. Cause me to fall in love with Your music. For when You come near, I am finally, forever, home.

⋄

As I wrapped up writing the final pages of this book, I revisited Dad's genealogical history, the one that began in the thirteenth century in St. Stephen-of-Brannel. And once again, I found a stunning detail I'd missed: "John Wallace Trethewey and family packed up and moved west somewhere between 1903 and 1906. They settled in Denver, Colorado, and lived at 455 E. 5th Ave . . . Perry Ross, their oldest son, started working as a millwright at mines in Colorado. Later he wrote a postcard to his parents from Breckenridge, Colorado, in 1907, saying that Jim, his younger brother, and himself were doing good."

Perry Ross Trethewey. Dad's grandfather and namesake. The one for whom he'd stand at the gate waiting for his copper mining shift to end. The same one who played checkers with him, provided a safe haven for him, and prayed for him.

This man who so impacted my history lived just a few short miles from where I now sit. And he worked as a miner in the mountain town I visit nearly every weekend.

I couldn't help but smile. With that seemingly small detail, the threads of so many complex stories in one family tree came together at long last. Although we were separated by continents and generations, the same God exhaled His presence and connected us all.

He'd been close all along in both the brokenness and the healing. He'd never left us, even when all we could feel was our pain. With more mercy and grace than I will ever comprehend, God never stopped pushing in, no matter the miles and mistakes. And with eyes alight with the glory of the God I love, I laughed with delight.

He *is* with us.

ALTAR STONE 12

LOOKING FOR GOD'S PRESENCE WITHIN YOU

It is often the most difficult to see what is closest to us. Case in point, the ketchup in the refrigerator and the broccoli in your teeth. The same could be said of the Holy Spirit's work. Those who follow Jesus have the Holy Spirit, the presence of God living in them. This means that regardless of whether you recognize Him, God is never far away. He's working in and through you to accomplish His purposes at all times, even while you sleep at night. But the story He's writing is bigger than your story. That means He's weaving the threads of your story and mine, the stories of generations before and after, to set up a kingdom of joy and peace and wholeness for all of eternity. Can you see evidence of God's presence in you, accomplishing His purposes for all humankind in your generation? There's a promised land coming, friend. Pray for God to open your eyes to see what you have missed. Then write it down. Mark it. This is your twelfth altar stone.

I learned that I couldn't change my past, but that I didn't have to be angry or victimized by it either. I could learn from it, change, and help others.

—DAD, DECEMBER 8, 2011

CONCLUSION

LIVING STONES

A GOD WHOSE PRESENCE IS EXPERIENCED WITH EACH OTHER

And the end of all our exploring
Will be to arrive where we started
And know the place for the first time.

—T. S. ELIOT, "LITTLE GIDDING"

I have found this in all the dark: we are all called to be witnesses.

—ANN VOSKAMP, *THE WAY OF ABUNDANCE*

NOVEMBER 6, 2014
11:36 A.M.

Michele,

We met at [the conference] and since then the Lord has put you on my heart again and again . . . Foolishly I thought it was just during the short season of your dad's death, but even as recently as Tuesday night, the Lord brought you to mind to pray for you.

I felt like a fish out of water at [the conference] . . . But I know that part of the reason I was there was to connect with you. You were a breath of fresh air, and our shared stories . . . made me feel normal.

This email puts you under *zero* obligation to write back, but after Tuesday night I felt obligated to let you know of my prayers for you.

In my vision I saw you in the midst of a huge metaphorical storm, and over and over again I saw a large hand reaching out to you. And I kept hearing that the Lord is near to you. (Psalm 34:18: "The Lord is near the brokenhearted; he is the Savior of those whose spirits are crushed down.") The Lord really wanted to impress upon me how precious you are to him and how he's for you, not against you. These aren't any remarkable words, but the Lord loves you so much, he's called me, a perfect stranger, to also tell you . . .

May God continue to use you mightily,

Nicholle

Nicholle's email is one of hundreds I've received over the years. But what you don't know and need to know is this:

First, Nicholle—by her own admission—was a stranger. She had zero insight into my daily reality, nor could she have predicted what life would look like for me over the years following her letter.

Second, the next day, November 7, 2014, at approximately 3:30 p.m. in the afternoon, my doctor called to inform me that cancer was back for the third time. Two weeks later, I lost my tongue—and my safe and familiar faith. The rest, as they say, is history. Much of that history is recorded in these pages.

And third, if I needed any more evidence of my God's relentless nearness than I've already documented, this letter would be it.

⋄

Two years later, again in November, I received a second email. This one came from the oncology nutrition specialist who kept me fed during the five months when all nourishment and fluid went through a gastrointestinal tube in my stomach. Although I had nothing but good memories of Sonya, seeing her name in my inbox brought back the nightmare.

> Hi Michele,
>
> It's been a long time. How are you? Totally feel free to ignore this email but there is going to be a research study coming up for patients going through treatment for head and neck cancer. They are putting together an advisory board to discuss ways to improve emotional well-being and all-around support for patients going through this particular type of treatment . . . I don't know if this is something you're interested in . . . but I immediately thought of you. Let me know if you get a chance.

I read the email two or three times trying to make sense of her invitation. A research study. For head and neck cancer patients. And they wanted me on the advisory board, a voice of experience to guide them through the process.

In subsequent emails, I found out that this particular study was being conducted by a large state university and that the results would go a long way toward developing mental-health support systems for those who experienced my particular kind of cancer. As a former registered nurse and an experienced patient, I understood the importance of this kind of research. But I didn't understand its importance to my future.

I wrote Sonya back that day and accepted her invitation. A few weeks later, I attended the first meeting.

It was dark when I pulled into the parking lot. Christmas was around the corner, but that night I traveled back in time. As I climbed out of my car and locked the doors, I looked over my right shoulder at the lights of St. Joseph's Hospital across the street. I recognized the covered entry, the red and white emergency room sign, the automatic glass doors, and the valet parking section for oncology patients. Two years before, I'd vomited into the garbage can by the front door before going in for what I hoped to be my final surgery.

My stomach flipped with the memory.

Turning my back on the hospital, I walked through the front doors and joined the meeting.

"You must be Michele." The woman in charge offered me a warm smile. "We're so glad you're here! Why don't you sit here by me?"

The table was covered with sodas, waters, and—thank You, Jesus—Qdoba. My favorite. But I felt too nervous to eat, not to mention hesitant to eat in front of people I didn't know. So I grabbed a water bottle and sat down next to our leader, trying to make myself invisible.

What followed over the next two hours proved pivotal to my healing.

Three former head and neck cancer patients attended, including myself. The other two shared their stories first—two men, one in his midforties, the other in his midfifties, best I could tell. One was a masters-level educator and the other a deputy with the police department. Both had survived throat cancer. And both were struggling to survive life after throat cancer. Depression, anxiety, substance abuse, relational challenges, PTSD at the most unexpected times. Neither could work, even though years had passed since their diagnosis. One spent his time volunteering with other cancer patients, an honest attempt to heal while doing life with others like him. The other was doing everything he could not to drink anymore and to hang on to his marriage.

I couldn't stop crying, no matter how hard I tried. Already chewed raw like ground beef, I resisted any more vulnerability. But the more they talked, the more I felt myself crack.

You see, for nearly two years, I'd believed something was wrong with me, that the grief and anger and nightmares were products of my weakness, my inability to get over cancer and move on with life. But through the honest revelations of two strangers, I discovered I wasn't the only one.

The lead researcher—a woman with PhD and various other letters after her name—explained to us that head and neck cancer is one of the most underresearched cancers. At the same time, head and neck cancer patients have the highest rates of anxiety, depression, substance abuse, and suicide.

I wasn't crazy. There wasn't something wrong with me.

Emboldened, I shared my story. The story of tongue cancer three times, countless surgeries, treatment that left me with a permanent disability, six children, three of whom come from their own trauma, surviving cancer only to fear succumbing to the life after cancer.

That's when their tears joined my own. I was undone. And in the process, I felt the first twinges of healing in a soul that had been rent in two.

The late Fred Rogers, Presbyterian minister and television personality who devoted his life to serving children, said these words: "Anything that's human is mentionable, and anything that is mentionable can be more manageable. When we can talk about our feelings, they become less overwhelming, less upsetting, and less scary. The people we trust with that important talk can help us know that we are not alone."[58]

This is what the university research study has done for me. It has validated my trauma by creating a space where I could tell the truth and has thereby subdued the internal screams through the presence and compassion of others.

It has been more than two years since I joined this board. Once a year, we meet to discuss the ongoing challenges of head and neck cancer patients and how best to create effective mental health strategies for those who are still in the dark of their battle. In the months between meetings, we email questions, suggestions, and strategies. We put flesh and blood and bone on what would be nothing more than ideas on paper without the pain of our experience. Because of that, the researchers are able to enter in and connect with people in places of suffering.

God bless them, they listen to us. They pay attention and take notes. They take what they learn from us—the ones who should've died and yet somehow survived—and do what they can to help those still fighting to live.

"The word *compassion*," writes Henri Nouwen, "is derived from the Latin words *pati* and *cum*, which together mean 'to suffer with.' Compassion asks us to go where it hurts, to enter into places of pain, to share in brokenness, fear, confusion, and anguish. Compassion challenges us to cry out with those in misery, to mourn with those who are lonely, to weep with those in tears. Compassion requires us to be weak with the weak, vulnerable with the vulnerable, and powerless with the powerless. Compassion means full immersion in the condition of being human."[59]

True compassion is full immersion. To recognize pain and refuse to walk past it. To sit down, get uncomfortable right there in another's writhing, and do what we can to bear it with them.

Sounds like covenant. Like the pillar of cloud and fire. The incarnation. The cross.

Doing this—doing what He did by entering in—will wreck us. And it will save us.

⁂

Go to places of suffering and be there.

Those were the words I heard twelve months ago when I started writing this book. It was the end of the year, when most people reflect on the months prior and plan for the year ahead. I was doing the same—evaluating past goals, setting new ones, asking God to give me wisdom and direction and then doing my darnedest to hear Him.

I wrote down a couple of no-brainer goals, things like run a 10k and set a date night once a quarter with my children. When you have six children, once a quarter is about all a mama can handle.

Go to places of suffering and be there.

I heard it again. It wasn't audible, like the sound of the oven timer going off or the blare of a horn. It was a gut feeling, a soul impression.

To tell the truth, I would've preferred something more tangible. Maybe a divine to-do list.

I thought of the multicultural Life Center opened by our church. Perhaps I could teach a class on public speaking or the craft of writing. Or maybe I could create an informal meeting space where friends and strangers could gather one night a week to drink coffee and share their questions about faith without fear of judgment.

Then I thought of the cancer centers and radiation oncology units where I'd spent so much time. Those were places of suffering, no doubt about it. Should I offer to spend time with those who were in the middle of treatment, maybe hold a hand or say a prayer?

I needed to *do* something. "Being there" didn't sound like much in the way of help. Hurting people need relief, answers, something that will help them get back to their lives, lives that promise happiness and fulfillment. Their promised land.

And yet as I look back over the twelve key markers in Scripture, the significant altar stones that mark the narrative and thesis of the Bible, the one consistent thread through all of them is God's presence. God going to places of suffering and *being there.*

With Adam and Eve in their garden and sin.

With Abraham in the cutting of the covenant.

With Jacob on his ladder and with his limp.

With the Israelites in their slavery and deliverance.

With Moses on a mountain and his people in the wilderness tabernacle.

With Elijah in his exhaustion and disillusionment.

With those searching for the Messiah but unable to see Him in a baby.

With John the Baptist in prison undeservedly and in doubt.

With the disciples who fell facedown as He revealed His glory.

With those who ate with Him but couldn't always make sense of Him.

With those who watched Him weep in a garden and die on a cross.

With those who sorrowed at His leaving and then celebrated with His Spirit.

He is in the middle of every hard part of the story, over and over again. Every time it looked as if the world would run off the rails, He entered. His relentless nearness cost him His reputation, His comfort, and His life. Even so, He pushed in.

Because God knew we need more than a God who will save us. We need a God who will be *with us*.

More than a year later, I think I finally understand, at least in part, God's heart for this hard season. I felt Him urge me to go to places of suffering and be there. Every time I tried to unravel the meaning of this urging, I assumed He wanted some kind of volunteerism, ministry, or service.

Then on a day when the emotions were raw and the thought of one more to-do made me want to collapse, I realized the place of suffering wasn't about volunteerism at all.

It was first about being willing to enter my own place of suffering. *With Him.*

He wanted me to go to the hard places in my story. The complicated relationship with my father. The marriage that ended in disillusionment and abandonment. The recurring cancer, the almost dying, and the lingering emotional and physical consequences of such a horrifying trauma. And the ongoing, daily struggle to stay present and tender with children trying to heal from their own pain.

To attempt to be present with others without first being tapped into the presence myself would be inauthentic at best, deceptive and dangerous at worst. Which is why working harder rarely makes me feel any better. As Thomas Merton so wisely penned, "He who attempts to act and do things for others or for the world without deepening his own self-understanding, freedom, integrity, and capacity to love will not have anything to give to others. He will communicate to them nothing but the contagion of his own obsessions, his aggressiveness, his ego-centered ambitions, his delusions about ends and means, his doctrinaire prejudices and ideas."[60]

If you open your Bible to Luke 5, you'll find a fishing story. Jesus is sitting in a boat with Simon Peter, a man who will soon become one of His disciples. And He tells him to throw his net to catch some fish. Peter resists, having fished all night with no results. What is one more cast going to accomplish? He is exhausted, hungry, ready to call it a day. He doesn't need one more thing to do. Even so, he complies. And within moments, the net that had remained empty through the night fills with so many fish it breaks.

Peter doesn't need a better boat, more skill, or a state-of-the-art fish finder. He doesn't need to polish his spirituality or find another ministry.

What he needs most of all? Jesus in the boat.

"Christ's presence confers success," theologian Charles Spurgeon writes. "Jesus sat in Peter's boat, and His will, by a mysterious influence, drew the fish to the net. When Jesus is lifted up in His Church, His presence is the Church's power—the shout of a king is in the midst of her."[61]

His presence is our power. And for reasons I will never fully understand, God chooses to deliver that incomparable power through flawed human children like you and me, men and women who have worked long through the night with little to show for it.

But when we invite Jesus into the boat, we're finally able to offer and experience what we never could manipulate on our own.

Healing. Of ourselves and each other.

In my years of unmoored faith, God stepped into all my grief and confusion and invited me to cast my net in His direction. He wanted me to trust, based on His character and consistent history, that although the proximity of my pain might blind me to Him, He would never leave. Whereas my efforts produced only more emptiness, He would fill any void with the balm of His presence.

Then and only then would I have something to offer someone else.

•≻◇≺•

I stood on the threshold of an old amphitheater, captivated. Spread out before me sat Gwennap Pit, a wide, grassy open-air theater carved into the Cornish hillside. And around its circumference sat the ghosts of thousands who'd come searching for faith in their places of pain. I could feel the memory of them, even if I couldn't see them.

Cornwall has a long history of copper and tin mining. (Those of you who are familiar with Winston Graham's twelve Poldark novels or the popular BBC series by the same name already know this.) It is believed Gwennap Pit formed as a result of a depression in the landscape over a collapsed mine. The fact that the pit doesn't collect water further suggests the likelihood of this.

But what interested me wasn't merely the mining history, although I knew that part of the story was tied up with mine. What captivated me was the fact that John Wesley—the founder of Methodism and an evangelist who shared the gospel with thousands all over England, Scotland, and Ireland—was said to have preached there.

Most historical accounts claim Wesley preached at Gwennap Pit at least seventeen times between 1762 and 1789, a favorite preaching venue because of its perfect acoustics and size. Although the amphitheater holds approximately two thousand people sitting comfortably, some records claim Wesley's biggest gathering at Gwennap topped a staggering thirty-two thousand, pulling in miners and their families who were hungry for hope in a life that was notorious for struggle.[62]

Wesley lived eighty-seven years, preaching until his final days, when he grew weak and could hardly speak. Seeing that he wanted to write final words but could not find the strength, an assistant offered to help.

"Let me write for you, sir; tell me what you would say," she said.

"Nothing," Wesley replied, "but that God is with us."[63]

But that God is with us.

As I stood on the edge of Gwennap Pit, Wesley's with-us God showed me just how close He stood. Hovering on the lip of the bowl, I could see how He'd weaved together the threads of my story with those of generations before. I looked at the grassy seats, now empty, knowing my ancestors—copper miners trying to earn a living and survive the suffering—likely joined the thirty-two thousand to hear the gospel preached in the late 1700s. By the 1800s, those ancestors had left their Cornish past for an American future, taking both their pain and faith with them to settle in Canada, Michigan, Colorado, and eventually Miami-Globe, Arizona, where in 1944 two young parents carrying their difficult childhoods and the death of their firstborn daughter brought into the world a scrawny, sickly boy who one day became my dad.

Two hundred years and five generations later, I stood on the same Cornish grass at Gwennap Pit, Trethewey blood flowing in my veins and hungry for the same Good News while trying to mine ore from the hard earth of my story.

I couldn't speak, could barely breathe. Directly across from where I stood were two white stones emerging from the kelly-green grass two-thirds up the opposite side.

"That's where he stood to preach," my friend Sherry said, noting my gaze. "John Wesley, the Methodist preacher. He stood in that spot when he shared the gospel."

I looked again at the white stones, now recognizing them as a preacher's pulpit.

With Wesley's legacy and my history pushing me forward, I made my way around Gwennap Pit's circumference. Then with one hand on each of the two pedestals, this gospel-loving girl whose speech and story will forever be flawed stepped up to stand between the remnants of a pulpit. And she knew in that moment she would never stop speaking about relentless love, no matter how broken she was.

Nothing but that God is with us.

Four years ago, I would've told you my biggest battle was fighting cancer and trying not to die. I now know otherwise.

The biggest battle I fought—and continue to fight—is the one for my faith. It's surviving the complexity of childhood and the suffering of adulthood without becoming blind to life's beauty. It's deciding to push in and trust when I want to pull back and self-protect. It's choosing relationship—over and over again, in spite of the risk—because I know true healing will always be found in connecting. And it's making space for mystery without letting my questions about God cloud what I know to be true about Him.

This has required me to become, like my ancestors, a miner of sorts. Someone willing to dig through the hard rock of my faith journey, unearthing stories and beliefs I'd long buried. And then to put each one through the white-hot fire of the gospel until everything false is burned up and only what is true remains.

The late pastor Eugene Peterson said, "When we submit our lives to what we read in scripture, we find that we are not being led to see God in our stories but our stories in God's. God is the larger context and plot in which our stories find themselves."[64]

I now know my suffering wasn't proof of God's punishment or absence. Instead, each impossibility provided a backdrop against which I could experience a new depth of God's reality. Although I still don't understand all the whys, His love for me cannot be denied. Now, moved by such a love, I pull these stones from the murky bottom of my Jordan River and set them up on the other side. The scars. The flawed speech. The tender emotions. The family that fights to be together. The fear of death. The longing for death.

Altar stones. Every one. And each testifies to the one who continues to carry me from the pain to the promised land. The altar of my life, as fragile and flawed as it is, bears witness. Not to my strength and determination to save myself. The dark nights that threatened to swallow me prove I lack both. Instead, the stones shout of a presence that pushes toward me when I no longer have the strength to reach toward Him. Then rather than walk a girl around her Jordan, He sometimes walks her through the middle of it. Because only then does she know how to enter into suffering with someone else.

I'll be stark-naked honest: I wish it weren't so hard.

I wish I always felt God's presence and affection. I wish the pain would end, the struggle would stop. And I wish the joy of living always outweighed the grief of it. This is now the miracle I pray for, that I will become a woman who laughs—big and loud—no matter what comes.

But I suspect this belly-jiggling joy will come only to the degree that I push in with Him. And to the degree that I remember His relentless love more than my dogged doubts.

The disciple Peter, the one so full of flaws and so full of Jesus-love, toward the end of his story said this: "As you come to him, the living Stone—rejected by humans but chosen by God and precious to him—you also, like living stones, are being built into a spiritual house to be a holy priesthood, offering spiritual sacrifices acceptable to God through Jesus Christ . . . But you are a chosen people, a royal priesthood, a holy nation, God's special possession, that you may declare the praises of him who called you out of darkness into his wonderful light" (1 Peter 2:4–5, 9).

Living stones that you may declare.

My friend, this is our mission. Not to work ourselves to death trying to be good enough to be loved. Not to get all of our religion right and hopefully win heaven. But to open our arms wide to the only love big enough to heal. Then when He pulls us from the darkness we thought we'd never escape, we stand as witnesses to Him.

God's presence, not our performance, is our glory.

We are recipients of grace, not manipulators of it. And our choosing to trust Him, to believe in His nearness no matter what comes, shines a light far brighter than any bootstrapped righteousness. This is when our stories find redemption, when those of us who nearly drowned in our Jordans reach out a hand to those still caught in the grip of theirs. There in the dark middle of another's suffering, our stones cast light, pointing to the relentless nearness of the one who is able to carry us through. Just as Joshua's stones became a memorial for generations to follow, our altar stones will help point the way for pilgrims who walk past us long after we're gone.

This is the truth and the grace.

Nothing but God with us.

Of all of author Philip Yancey's works, *Soul Survivor* stands as my favorite. In it, Philip identifies thirteen unlikely mentors who helped his faith survive the church. Through pen and pages, he invited me into the disappointments of a faith and followers who failed him. And then he shared how thirteen imperfect individuals helped him heal from the pain other imperfect individuals rent. In the epilogue he summates his list of spiritual guides with bare honesty and affection.

"As I review the list in total," he writes, "I see flawed, not perfect people. Several of them, a psychiatrist would probably diagnose as unstable. Each one had longings that went unfulfilled, dreams that never entered reality. I learn from them how to handle my own longings . . . Soren Kierkegaard said, 'With the help of the thorn in my foot, I spring higher than anyone with sound feet.' Some of the people profiled in this collection demonstrate that proverb as well. I would add only that we also need the help of those who show us what direction to spring."[65]

During these recent tumultuous years, Yancey became one of those imperfect voices shedding light on my faith. My father is also one of those flawed spiritual mentors, even in his absence. Now it's my turn to offer a hand to someone else. And yours.

You and I serve as living reminders of the never-failing, never-ending, relentless presence of God. As living stones, we bear witness each time we face impossible circumstances and receive mercy enough to overcome. Our dogged trust—no matter how bruised and tattered—lends strength to those who doubt and despair. And with each hand extended to one drowning in the dark, we testify to the only truth solid enough to pull us both through: God has not abandoned us. His presence is unshakeable, and He will never let us go until the day He finally brings us home.

"I will not leave you as orphans; I will come to you," He promised.

And I believe Him.

Now that's something worth living for.

Recommended Reading List

Several voices offered counsel, hard-earned perspective, and the warmth of their compassion through my season of spiritual darkness. Although I never met a single one of them—which would be impossible for three because they are no longer living—their words kept vigil with me during some of my most tender moments.

Knowing that you, too, might need a mentor or two one day, I've included their names and books here. It's important to note that not all of these authors or writings come from a Christian or biblical perspective. And I didn't necessarily agree with every author or every word. Even so, I will always be grateful for their companionship and guidance. And I'm honored now to make this introduction between friends.

Cloud, Henry. *Changes That Heal.*

Keller, Timothy. *Prayer.*

———. *The Reason for God.*

———. *Walking with God through Pain and Suffering.*

Lewis, C. S. *A Grief Observed.*

———. *The Weight of Glory.*

Manning, Brennan. *Abba's Child.*

———. *The Furious Longing of God.*

———. *The Ragamuffin Gospel.*

———. *The Relentless Tenderness of Jesus.*

Nakazawa, Donna Jackson. *Childhood Disrupted.*

Nouwen, Henri J. M. *The Inner Voice of Love.*

———. *The Return of the Prodigal Son.*
———. *Wounded Healer.*
Ortberg, John. *Soul Keeping.*
Taylor, Barbara Brown. *An Altar in the World.*
———. *Learning to Walk in the Dark.*
Van der Kolk, Bessel. *The Body Keeps the Score.*
Willard, Dallas. *Living in Christ's Presence.*
Yancey, Philip. *The Question That Never Goes Away*
———. *Soul Survivor.*
———. *What Good Is God?*

For more recommended books and free
resources to support you in your spiritual journey,
go to **MicheleCushatt.com/Resources**

Questions for Group Discussion or Personal Reflection

Introduction: The Twelve Stones

1. "Presence lends us courage to persist" (p. 17). Think of a difficult time in your life when someone came alongside you at a key moment. It could be the day you started a new job, a 5K you ran with a friend, a neighbor you met after you moved to a new state, the greeter who welcomed you at the church's front door, and so on. How did presence make a difference for you?
2. Consider the dual meaning of the title of this book: *Relentless*. Life can often feel like a long series of unending crises and difficulties. It's exhausting. The premise of this book, however, is that God's presence is even more relentless than your most relentless struggle. No matter how exhaust*ing* the living, His love and presence are exhaust*ive*. What does this mean for you?
3. The subtitle of *Relentless* is "The Unshakeable Presence of a God Who Never Leaves." Have you ever experienced a time when God felt absent and you wondered whether He had left you?
4. What do you hope to learn, gain, or discover while reading *Relentless*? Share it as a prayer.

Chapter 1: A Garden: A God Who Has Always Wanted to Be with You

1. Ordinary childhood memories can be some of the sweetest. What is one of your favorite everyday memories from early childhood?
2. "Reciprocity is key to vibrant relationship" (p. 31). The word "reciprocity" comes from the Latin *reciprocus,* which means "moving back and forth." Simply, it's the practice of mutual exchange, action, or influence. Give and take. Responsiveness. How do you see reciprocity (or the lack of it) playing out in your most important relationships?
3. Why do you think reciprocity is important to thriving relationships?
4. Take a few moments to consider "Altar Stone 1: Looking for Evidence of God in the Beginning of Your Story." What hints of God's nearness do you see in your earliest memories?

Chapter 2: A Smoking Firepot and a Blazing Torch: A God Who Promises to Be with You

1. I was seven years old when I decided to make a public declaration of my faith in Jesus. Although I was young, I remember the day well. Do you remember the day you first believed in God? Briefly share the story.
2. God is a promise-keeping God. His perfect, holy nature does not allow Him to be otherwise. What does it mean to you to know that God will always keep His word?
3. Hebrews 13:5 says, "Never will I leave you; never will I forsake you," a reference to God's promise of presence to Joshua in Deuteronomy 31:6. If God is a promise-keeping God, this means His presence with us is absolute. We can count on it. Does your life reflect this level of absolute confidence in God's never-failing presence?

Chapter 3: A Ladder and a Limp: A God Who Meets You Where You Are

1. Jacob, a man who would one day be the patriarch of the twelve tribes of Israel, had a story riddled with mistakes. And yet God chose him to be a leader of His people. Does this give you any comfort, and how so?
2. What new insight about yourself and your family of origin did you gain in reading Jacob's story?
3. Chapter 3 begins with the humorous story of the third-grade note-passing incident. My blunder was minor and certainly not worth lost sleep. But I was devastated. Even at eight years old, I believed my mistake pushed me beyond redemption. And my shame over that incident followed me for years. How about you? Is there a failure in your early years that nags you?
4. The subtitle of this chapter is "A God Who Meets You Where You Are." How has God met you where you are, even if you aren't where you thought you'd be?

Chapter 4: A Pillar of Cloud and Fire: A God Who Is with You When You Wander

1. At the beginning of chapter 4, I mention visiting the Mother Cabrini Shrine in Denver, Colorado, in my quest to feel close to God. Although there is nothing magical about a place of worship or a memorial, there are times when a particular chair, chapel, prayer walk, mountain hike, labyrinth, park, or shrine lends us both space and quiet as we attempt to focus our attention on God. Do you have a place you like to visit in your pursuit of God's presence?
2. The story of the Israelites is one of my favorites, chiefly because they never seemed to escape their dysfunctional patterns. Generation after generation, they kept making the same mistakes. Although God corrected them, He never stopped loving

them. His affection remained steadfast, even when their faith didn't. What does this mean to you?

3. Review the attachment styles mentioned on pages 74–75. Which of the three attachment styles do you most identify with? How do you see your attachment style playing out in your primary relationships? How do you see it playing out in your relationship with God?

Chapter 5: A Tabernacle: A God Whose Mercy Carries You

1. What are some prayer practices that have helped you to connect with God?
2. The tabernacle was temporary. It was never intended to be the sole means to humanity's connection with God. The same is true for us today. We don't need to enter a tent or building to draw near to God's presence, nor is God's presence accessible only on Sundays. What does this mean for you?
3. At the beginning of this chapter, I shared the story of well-intentioned church leaders who wounded me and, as a result, marred my spiritual journey. The means of their "confrontation" created a stumbling block in my relationship with God. How about you? What formative experiences have colored your spiritual journey and perception of God?

Chapter 6: A Cleft in a Rock: A God Who Is with You When You Reach the End of Yourself

1. How can we "feed" and "touch" those who suffer in much the way God ministered to Elijah in his suffering?
2. Have you ever felt the pressure—either within or without—to appear stronger and more confident and optimistic in your faith than you actually feel?
3. Have you ever reached the "end of yourself?" What did you learn in that season?

4. With prayer and a keen eye, spend some time considering that season. What glimpses do you see of God's nearness with you, even if you couldn't feel Him at the time? How did He feed you and touch you when you needed Him most?

Chapter 7: An Incarnation: A God Who Is with You in Your Humanity

1. Read Romans 8:31–39 out loud. Compare and contrast God's love with human love.
2. Do you believe your weaknesses are a turn-off to God? Why or why not? What about those mistakes you make over and over again?
3. Pain is a powerful teacher, whether that time you burned your finger on the stove or when your school friend talked about you behind your back. What are some of the lessons you've learned from pain, big or small, seen or unseen?

Chapter 8: A Prison: A God Who Is with You in Your Doubt

1. Have you ever experienced doubt—big or small—in your faith journey? What caused the seed of doubt? And what specifically did you doubt about God?
2. Have you ever experienced a miracle? Being mindful of the time and others in your group, briefly share your experience. How did it impact your faith?
3. Have you ever prayed for a miracle but didn't receive one? Again, being mindful of the time and others in your group, share your experience. How did it impact your faith?

Chapter 9: A Transfiguration: A God Who Is with You in Your Transformation

1. At the beginning of this chapter, I talked about my love of sports, NFL football in particular. What is something you enjoy that others might be surprised to know about you?

2. Imagine what would happen if, for an entire day, your home, church, school, or office said no to grace and embraced only truth, all the way. Get specific. What would that day look like?
3. Now do the opposite. Imagine what would happen if, for an entire day, your community rejected all truth and instead embraced 100 percent grace. What would that day look like?
4. "What man can disfigure, God can transfigure" (p. 156). How is God transfiguring something in your story that is broken and scarred?

Chapter 10: A Meal: A God Who Is with You in Your Hunger

1. Many cultural traditions center around food and meals. What is one food-related tradition that is important to you? Why?
2. Besides physical hunger, what are you most "hungry" for right now?
3. Read Psalm 90:14 and Isaiah 55:1–2 out loud. Several times in Scripture the presence of God is associated with satisfying our hunger. What are some signs of spiritual hunger? What does it look like? What does it feel like?

Chapter 11: A Cross: A God Who Is with You in Pain, Suffering, and Death

1. Take a moment to make a list of everything we have at our disposal that can help us numb or avoid pain (of any kind). Do you think this helps us or hurts us?
2. Families are complicated, even the best ones. And like my dad and myself, even the most well-intentioned family members don't get it all right. How does this encourage you in your journey?
3. On page 21 in the introduction, I included the following quote by John Ortberg: "If you ask people who don't believe in God why they don't, the number one reason will be suffering. If you ask people who believe in God when they grew most spiritually, the number one answer will be suffering." Have you discovered this paradox to be true?

Chapter 12: An Indwelling: A God Whose Presence Lives in You

1. If you could pick one song as the anthem of your life, what would it be? If you're feeling particularly brave, sing it for your group!
2. If you and I had full access to all the cash in a bank, we wouldn't hesitate to take it. We'd probably rush to be the first in line. Through the Holy Spirit, we have full and direct access to God's presence, twenty-four hours a day, seven days a week. He's worth far more than any bank can buy. And yet we rarely take advantage of it. Why do you think this is?
3. There are many descriptions for the Holy Spirit in the Bible, including Spirit of the Father, Teacher, Spirit of Adoption, Comforter, Counselor, Spirit of Truth, Spirit of Life, Spirit of Holiness, and so on. Which name means the most to you? Why?

Conclusion: Living Stones: A God Whose Presence Is Experienced with Each Other

1. How might your altar stones cast light for others in places of darkness, both now and in generations to come?
2. Trying to minister to others without first allowing the presence of God to minister to us is like trying to do CPR on someone while holding our breath. Both people will be hurt in the process. Think of a time when you tried to do "God's work" without being connected to God Himself. What happened?
3. As you reflect on this journey through your story and God's story together, what is your biggest takeaway? How are you different as a result of what God has revealed to you?

For a more comprehensive reading guide for small group discussion or Bible study groups, visit **www.MicheleCushatt.com/Relentless**

Notes

1. Nadia Kounang, "What You Need to Know about Fentanyl," CNN .com, November 5, 2018, https://www.cnn.com/2016/05/10/health/fentanyl-opioid-explainer/index.html.
2. Ann Voskamp, *The Way of Abundance: A Sixty-Day Journey into a Deeply Meaningful Life* (Grand Rapids: Zondervan, 2018).
3. Brennan Manning, *The Ragamuffin Gospel: Good News for the Bedraggled, Beat-Up, and Burnt Out* (Colorado Springs: Multnomah, 2005), 30.
4. John Ortberg, *Soul Keeping: Caring for the Most Important Part of You* (Grand Rapids: Zondervan, 2014).
5. Philip Yancey, *Soul Survivor: How Thirteen Unlikely Mentors Helped My Faith Survive the Church* (New York: Doubleday, 2001), 5.
6. Ibid.
7. John Calvin, *The Institutes of the Christian Religion*, book 1, *The Knowledge of the Creator*, trans. Henry Beveridge (London: Bonham Norton, 1599), 1.1, https://www.reformed.org/books/institutes/books/book1/bk1ch01.html.
8. Thomas á Kempis, *The Imitation of Christ*, book 2, chapter 8 (Milwaukee: Bruce Publishing Company, 1940), 65–66.
9. Dana Bartholomew, "Sylmar–San Fernando Earthquake: Forty-Five Years Ago Tuesday, Sixty-Four Killed," *Los Angeles Daily News*, February 8, 2016, https://www.dailynews.com/2016/02/08/sylmar-san-fernando-earthquake-45-years-ago-tuesday-64-killed/.
10. K. Baltzer, *The Covenant Formulary* (Philadelphia: Fortress Press, 1971); G. E. Mendenhall, "Covenant Forms in Israelite Tradition," *Biblical Archaeologist* 17 (1954): 50–76; E. F. Campbell Jr. and D. N. Freedman, eds., *The Biblical Archaeologist Reader* 3, (repr., Garden City, NY: Doubleday, 1970): 25–53; M. Weinfeld, "berîth," *Theological Dictionary of the New Testament*, ed. G. Johannes Botterweck and Helmer Ringgren, trans. John T. Willis et al., vol. 2, rev. ed. (Grand Rapids: Eerdmans, 1977): 253–79.
11. S. B. Cowan, "Covenant," in *Holman Illustrated Bible Dictionary*, ed. C. Brand et al. (Nashville: Holman Bible Publishers, 2003), 355–56.

12. Robert Putnam, *Bowling Alone: The Collapse and Revival of American Community* (New York: Simon and Schuster, 2001).
13. John T. Cacioppio and William Patrick, *Loneliness: Human Nature and the Need for Social Connection* (New York: Norton, 2008).
14. Russell D. Moore, *The Storm-Tossed Family: How the Cross Reshapes the Home* (Nashville: Broadman and Holman, 2018).
15. See http://www.mothercabrinishrine.org/.
16. Parker J. Palmer, *A Hidden Wholeness: The Journey toward an Undivided Life* (San Francisco: Jossey-Bass, 2004).
17. See "About the CDC-Kaiser ACE Study," CDC website, https://www.cdc.gov/violenceprevention/acestudy/about.html.
18. Donna Jackson Nakazawa, *Childhood Disrupted: How Your Biography Becomes Your Biology, and How You Can Heal* (New York: Atria/Simon and Schuster, 2015), 15, 32.
19. See *Online Etymology Dictionary,* s.v. "aloof," https://www.etymonline.com/word/aloof.
20. Henri J. M. Nouwen, *The Wounded Healer: Ministry in Contemporary Society* (New York: Doubleday/Random House, 1972), 77–78.
21. Nakazawa, *Childhood Disrupted.*
22. Barbara Brown Taylor, *Learning to Walk in the Dark* (New York: HarperOne, 2014), 108.
23. R. A. Cole, *Exodus: An Introduction and Commentary*, vol. 2 (Downers Grove, IL: InterVarsity, 1973), 234.
24. W. A. Elwell and B. J. Beitzel, "Mercy Seat," in *Baker Encyclopedia of the Bible*, vol. 2 (Grand Rapids: Baker, 1988), 1441.
25. Timothy Keller, "The Still Small Voice," *Timothy Keller Sermons Podcast by Gospel in Life*, June 30, 2016, https://itunes.apple.com/us/podcast/timothy-keller-sermons-podcast-by-gospel-in-life/id352660924?mt=2&i=1000371718377.
26. John Piper, "Come to Church Desperate," DesiringGod.org, June 24, 2018, https://www.desiringgod.org/articles/come-to-church-desperate.
27. Bessel van der Kolk, *The Body Keeps the Score: Brain, Mind, and Body in the Healing of Trauma* (New York: Penguin, 2014), 81.
28. Henri J. M. Nouwen, *The Inner Voice of Love: Journey through Anguish to Freedom* (New York: Doubleday/Random House, 1996), 49.
29. Van der Kolk, *The Body Keeps the Score*, 113.
30. *Merriam-Webster*, s.v. "attune," https://www.merriam-webster.com/dictionary/attune.

31. Lindsey O'Connor wrote a poignant and thought-provoking memoir detailing her experience of near-death during childbirth and her long road to recovery, in body and identity and in her relationship with the daughter she birthed but struggled to know. It's titled *The Long Awakening* (Grand Rapids: Revell, 2013), and I highly recommend it.
32. Spiros Zodhiates, Warren Baker, Tim Rake, and David Kemp, *The Hebrew-Greek Key Word Study Bible, NIV Version* (Chattanooga: AMG International, 1996), 4997.
33. Kate Bowler, *Everything Happens for a Reason: And Other Lies I've Loved* (New York: Random House, 2018).
34. Manning, *Ragamuffin Gospel*, 115–16.
35. Frederick Buechner, *Wishful Thinking: A Theological ABC* (New York: Harper and Row, 1973).
36. Leonard Sweet, Twitter post, October 8, 2018, https://twitter.com/lensweet/status/1049264649869262848.
37. Augustine of Hippo, *Of Grace and Free Will*, x.
38. Matthew Henry, *Matthew Henry's Commentary on the Whole Bible: Complete and Unabridged in One Volume* (Peabody, MA: Hendrickson, 1994), 1665.
39. Henry Cloud, *Changes That Heal* (Grand Rapids: Zondervan, 1992), 25.
40. Ibid.
41. Andy Stanley, "The Bible according to Jesus: Fully Filled," FaithGateway.com, September 9, 2018, https://www.faithgateway.com/bible-according-jesus/.
42. Edward Mote, "My Hope Is Built on Nothing Less" (1834).
43. *Merriam-Webster*, s.v. "disfigure," https://www.merriam-webster.com/dictionary/disfigure.
44. *Macmillan Dictionary*, s.v. "disfigure," https://www.macmillandictionary.com/us/dictionary/american/disfigure.
45. *Merriam-Webster*, s.v. "transfigure," https://www.merriam-webster.com/dictionary/transfigure.
46. Ibid.
47. "The Last Supper—by Leonardo Da Vinci," Leonardo Da Vinci website, https://www.leonardodavinci.net/the-last-supper.jsp. See also "The Last Supper and Santa Maria delle Grazie," LeonardoAMilano.com website, http://www.leonardoamilano.org/english/last_supper.php.
48. D. Brack, "Table Fellowship," in *The Lexham Bible Dictionary*, ed. J. D. Barry et al. (Bellingham, WA: Lexham Press, 2016).

49. "Harry F. Harlow, Monkey Love Experiments," Adoption History Project, University of Oregon, https://pages.uoregon.edu/adoption/studies/HarlowMLE.htm.
50. Zodhiates et al., *Hebrew-Greek Key Word Study Bible*, 1544.
51. Ibid., 1535–36.
52. Manning, *Ragamuffin Gospel*, 167.
53. Henri J. M. Nouwen, *Turn My Mourning into Dancing* (Nashville: Thomas Nelson, 2004), 96.
54. For those interested in learning more about Debi Grebenik and the Trauma Training Institute, you can find information at https://traumatraininginstitute.com/ or connect with her on her professional Facebook page at www.facebook.com/TraumaTrainingInstitute/.
55. Debi Grebenik tells me that this dog bite analogy originated with Dr. Daniel Siegel's excellent work, particularly his book *The Mindful Therapist: A Clinician's Guide to Mindsight and Neural Integration* (New York: Norton, 2010), 169.
56. While this is a well-supported therapeutic approach to helping children heal from trauma, it's important to note that this does not mean blanket subjection to abuse and threats of harm. When trauma responses turn dangerous or when self-harm or violence is threatened, outside intervention and support are required.
57. Charles Spurgeon, *Morning and Evening, KJV Edition* (Peabody, MA: Hendrickson, 1991), April 25.
58. Fred Rogers, 1969 Senate Hearing, PBS Kids, https://www.youtube.com/watch?v=J9uIJ-o2yqQ.
59. Henri J. M. Nouwen, *Compassion: A Reflection on the Christian Life* (New York: Image Books, 1983), 4.
60. Thomas Merton, *Thomas Merton, Spiritual Master: The Essential Writings* (Mahwah, NJ: Paulist Press, 1992), 375.
61. Spurgeon, *Morning and Evening,* October 8.
62. See https://www.cornwalls.co.uk/history/gwennap_pit.htm; see also https://www.britainexpress.com/counties/cornwall/churches/gwennap-pit.htm.
63. Stephen Tomkins, *John Wesley: A Biography* (Grand Rapids: Eerdmans, 2003), 193–94.
64. Eugene Peterson, *Eat This Book: A Conversation in the Art of Spiritual Reading* (Grand Rapids: Eerdmans, 2009), 44.
65. Yancey, *Soul Survivor*, 319.

DISCOVER MICHELE'S PREVIOUSLY RELEASED BOOKS

Undone is author Michele Cushatt's quest to make peace with a complicated life. It is an honest confession of a diagnosis of cancer and the joys and disappointments of motherhood and marriage, ripe with regret over what is and, yet, still hopeful for what could be.

In the end, *Undone* turns complication into a beautiful canvas, angst into joy, and the unknown into an adventure, revealing that sometimes life's most colorful and courageous stories are written right in the middle of the mess.

When a brutal bout with cancer changed how she looked, talked, and lived, Michele embarked on a soul-deep journey to rediscover herself.

With raw personal stories, rock-solid biblical teaching, and radical truths on which to rebuild your life, *I Am* reminds us that our value isn't found in our talents, achievements, relationships, or appearance. It is instead found in a God who chose us, sent us, and promised to be with us—forever.

For free premium resources for these books visit MicheleCushatt.com/resources

FOR MORE OF

RELENTLESS

AUDIO BOOK

Listen to Michele read *Relentless* on audio, including bonus content you can't get anywhere else woven throughout.

Download it on Audible or your favorite audio book retailer.

The RELENTLESS PODCAST *with Michele Cushatt*

Michele recorded a brand new season of her podcast specifically for *Relentless*. In each episode, she dives deeper into the core concept and story of that chapter, helping you rediscover the presence of a God who never leaves.

Listen in on iTunes, Google Play or any of your favorite podcast platforms.

For more information on these and other *Relentless* resources, go to www.MicheleCushatt.com/relentless.